GUINNESS WORLD RECORDS

Record-Breaking Comprehension
Year 5

Teacher's Book
Gill Howell

Published by
RISING★STARS
in association with
GUINNESS WORLD RECORDS

Rising Stars UK Ltd. part of Hodder Education, an Hachette UK Company
Carmelite House, 50 Victoria Embankment, London, EC4Y 0DZ
www.risingstars-uk.com

Every effort has been made to trace copyright holders and obtain their permission for the use of copyright materials. The author and publisher will gladly receive information enabling them to rectify any error or omission in subsequent editions. All facts are correct at the time of going to press. All referenced websites were correct at the time this book went to press.

Text, design and layout © Rising Stars UK Ltd.

The right of Gill Howell to be identified as the author of this work has been asserted by her in accordance with the Copyright, Design and Patents Act 1998.

Published 2013
Reprinted 2013 (twice), 2014, 2015 (twice)
All underlying records data © Guinness World Records Ltd.

Published in association with Guinness World Records.

Author: Gill Howell
Text design: Burville-Riley Partnership/Words & Pictures Ltd
Typesetting: Words & Pictures Ltd
Cover design: Burville-Riley Partnership
Publisher: Becca Law
Project manager: Tracey Cowell
Editor: Jennie Clifford

Photo acknowledgements
Page 9: rheo/iStockphoto; **page 11**: © nmcandre/iStockphoto; **page 13**: 4x6/iStockphoto; **page 15**: © Helga Jaunegg/iStockphoto; **page 17**: © Kuzma/iStockphoto; **page 19**: cenkeratila/iStockphoto; **page 21**: © ihor_seamless/iStockphoto; **page 23**: omergenc/iStockphoto; **page 33**: © leontura/iStockphoto; **page 35**: © House@Brasil Art Studio/iStockphoto; **page 39**: © Frank Ramspott/iStockphoto; **page 41**: © chieferu/iStockphoto; **page 49**: © sumografika/iStockphoto; **page 53**: © kayann/iStockphoto; **page 55**: © creacion/iStockphoto.
Rising Stars is grateful to Guinness World Records for supplying all of the record-related pictures in the book.

All rights reserved. No part of this publication may be reproduced, stored in a retrieval system, or transmitted, in any form by any means, electronic, mechanical, photocopying, recording or otherwise, without the prior permission of Rising Stars.

British Library Cataloguing in Publication Data.
A CIP record for this book is available from the British Library.
ISBN: 978-0-85769-569-7

Printed by Ashford Colour Press

CONTENTS

How to use this book 4

Content summary grid 6

Most pairs in a three-legged race 8

Longest career as a weather forecaster 10

Largest bhangra dance 12

Most guide dogs trained by an organisation 14

Farthest distance limbo-skating under cars 16

Youngest male to row an ocean solo 18

Hottest chilli 20

Most skateboard nollies in 30 seconds 22

Largest hands 24

Fastest talker 26

Tallest teenager living (male) 28

Largest vertical garden (green wall) 30

Largest hairy family 32

Heaviest vehicle pulled by hair (female) 34

Largest gathering of people dressed as leprechauns 36

Most decks of playing cards memorised – single sighting 38

Largest torchlit parade 40

Longest fingernails (female) – ever 42

Shortest living woman 44

Largest drumming lesson 46

Deepest scuba dive in sea water 48

Strangest diet 50

Largest gymnastic display (female) 52

Largest atlas 54

Notes 56

GUINNESS WORLD RECORDS

RECORD-BREAKING COMPREHENSION – YEAR 5

HOW TO USE THIS BOOK

Record-Breaking Comprehension is a brand new resource that uses the appeal of Guinness World Records to engage pupils in reading comprehension texts.

The records are described via a range of fiction and non-fiction text types, including newspaper reports, instructional web pages, blog entries and letters. The grid on pages 6–7 summarises the text types covered.

This Teacher's Book provides:

- answers to the questions, plus guidance on AFs and question types covered;

- support and research pointers for the Beyond the Record activities;

- photocopiable activities for writing, speaking and listening, linked to each record.

Reading comprehension questions

The reading comprehension questions in the Pupil Book are split into three differentiated sections: On your marks, Get set and Go for gold! The questions within each section become increasingly more challenging. For Years 3 and 4, there are three questions in each section; this increases to four questions per section for Years 5 and 6. You may wish to ask different groups of children to answer a particular set, or sets, of questions, depending on their ability.

The questions cover a range of AFs and question types (literal, inference, deduction and personal opinion), details of which can be found with the answers. A summary of coverage can be found on the grid on pages 6–7.

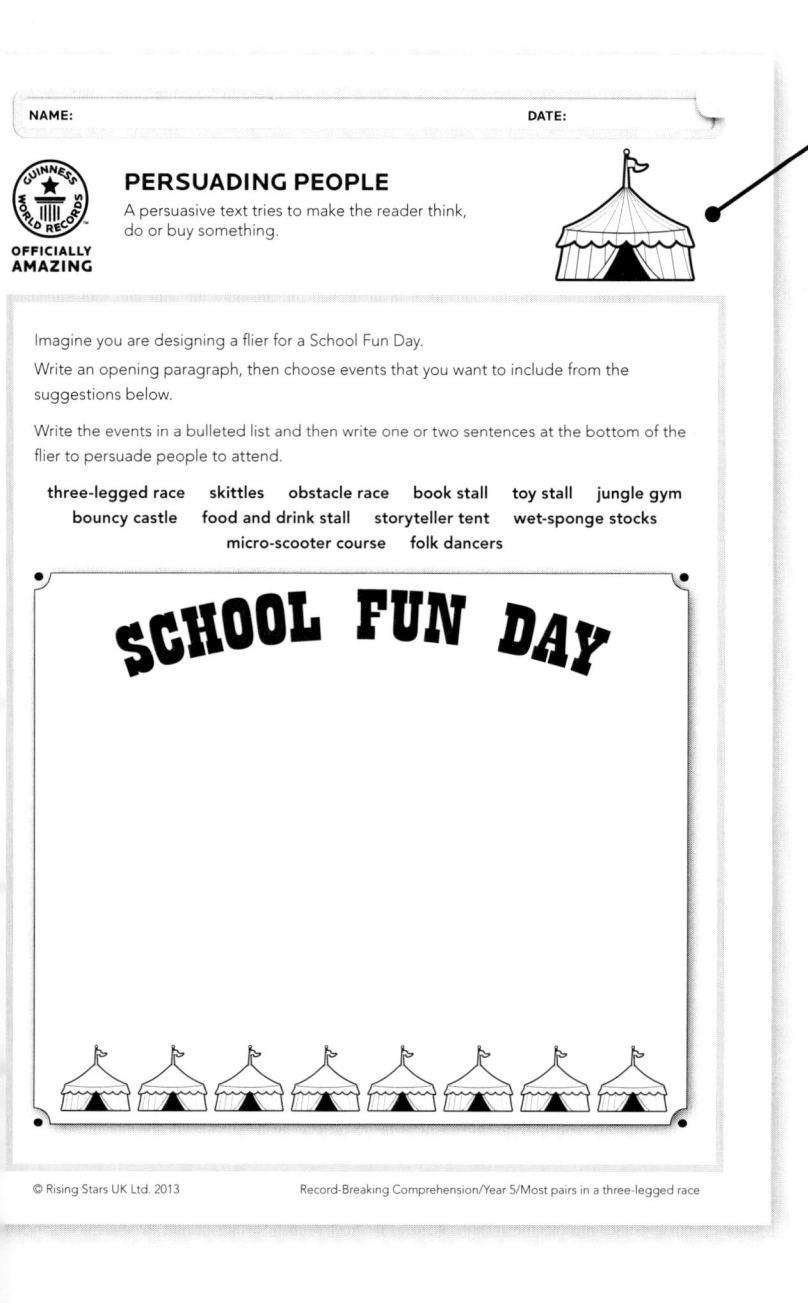

Language activity worksheets

Each of the photocopiable activity worksheets focuses on different language features and skills that children need to develop within the year group, and includes grammar, spelling and punctuation activities. There are suggestions for how to introduce each worksheet, as well as teaching prompts. A summary of the coverage for the worksheets can be found in the grid on pages 6–7.

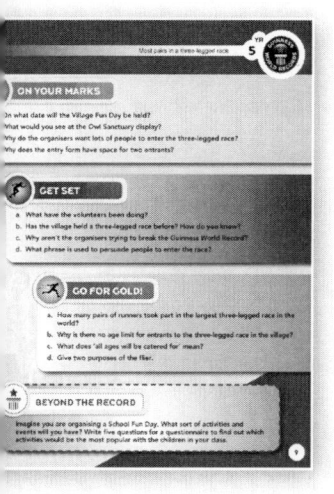

NAME: **DATE:**

PERSUADING PEOPLE
A persuasive text tries to make the reader think, do or buy something.

Imagine you are designing a flier for a School Fun Day.

Write an opening paragraph, then choose events that you want to include from the suggestions below.

Write the events in a bulleted list and then write one or two sentences at the bottom of the flier to persuade people to attend.

three-legged race   skittles   obstacle race   book stall   toy stall   jungle gym
bouncy castle   food and drink stall   storyteller tent   wet-sponge stocks
micro-scooter course   folk dancers

SCHOOL FUN DAY

© Rising Stars UK Ltd. 2013   Record-Breaking Comprehension/Year 5/Most pairs in a three-legged race

Beyond the record

These follow-up activities can be used with any child, regardless of their level and progress through the reading comprehension questions. Many of the activities involve children researching more about the record and presenting their findings.

Each activity is accompanied by structured teacher's notes, including web references where appropriate. The activities can be used both for class work and homework.

5

GUINNESS WORLD RECORDS

RECORD-BREAKING COMPREHENSION – YEAR 5

CONTENT SUMMARY GRID

Record title	Text type	AF coverage	Worksheet focus
Most pairs in a three-legged race	Flier: persuasion	AF2, AF3, AF5, AF6	Persuasive texts
Longest career as a weather forecaster	Web page: explanation/recount	AF2, AF3, AF5	Dictionary use
Largest bhangra dance	Diary: recount	AF2, AF3, AF5, AF6, AF7	Suffixes
Most guide dogs trained by an organisation	Flier: persuasion	AF2, AF3, AF4, AF5, AF6	Relative clauses
Farthest distance limbo-skating under cars	Newspaper: recount	AF2, AF3, AF4, AF5	Suffixes
Youngest male to row an ocean solo	Book: recount/non-chronological report	AF2, AF3, AF5, AF6	Identifying key information in a text
Hottest chilli	Book: instructions/non-chronological report	AF2, AF3, AF4, AF5, AF7	Homophones
Most skateboard nollies in 30 seconds	Magazine: instructions	AF2, AF3, AF4, AF5, AF7	Homophones and other words that sound similar
Largest hands	Flier: instructions/non-chronological report	AF2, AF3, AF6, AF7	Bullet points
Fastest talker	Web page: non-chronological report	AF2, AF3, AF4, AF5	Proofreading
Tallest teenager living (male)	Book: explanation	AF2, AF3, AF4, AF5	Commas and connectives
Largest vertical garden (green wall)	Book: explanation/instructions	AF2, AF3, AF5, AF6	Prefixes
Largest hairy family	Book: explanation	AF2, AF3, AF5	Latin words
Heaviest vehicle pulled by hair (female)	Magazine: instructions/recount	AF2, AF3, AF4, AF5, AF7	Connectives

GUINNESS WORLD RECORDS

RECORD-BREAKING COMPREHENSION – YEAR 5

Record title	Text type	AF coverage	Worksheet focus
Largest gathering of people dressed as leprechauns	Character sketch/legend	AF2, AF3, AF5, AF6, AF7	Synonyms
Most decks of playing cards memorised – single sighting	Web page: instructions	AF2, AF3, AF4, AF5	Acrostics for spelling
Largest torchlit parade	Magazine: explanation	AF2, AF3, AF5	Hyphens
Longest fingernails (female) – ever	Email: biography	AF2, AF3, AF5	Compound words
Shortest living woman	Magazine: biography	AF2, AF3, AF5, AF6	Direct speech
Largest drumming lesson	Newsletter: recount	AF2, AF3, AF5, AF6	Active and passive voice
Deepest scuba dive in sea water	Magazine: recount	AF2, AF3, AF7	Spelling
Strangest diet	Book: biography	AF2, AF3, AF5, AF6	Homophones
Largest gymnastic display (female)	Travel guide: non-chronological report	AF2, AF3, AF5, AF6	Synonyms
Largest atlas	Web page: non-chronological report	AF2, AF3, AF5	Active and passive voice

7

GUINNESS WORLD RECORDS

RECORD-BREAKING COMPREHENSION – YEAR 5

MOST PAIRS IN A THREE-LEGGED RACE

This text is in the form of a flier inviting people from the local community to enter the Village Fun Day. It is based on the record for the most pairs in a three-legged race.

Text type:	persuasion
AFs covered:	AF2, AF3, AF5, AF6
Specialist vocabulary:	volunteer, festivities, sanctuary, competitor, performance

ON YOUR MARKS

a. The Village Fun Day will be held on 28 July. *Literal AF2*
b. You would see different types of owls flying at the Owl Sanctuary display. *Deduction AF3*
c. The organisers want lots of people to enter the three-legged race so they will break the village record. *Inference AF3*
d. There is space on the form for two entrants because two people are needed to run in a three-legged race. *Deduction AF3*

GET SET

a. The volunteers have been preparing for the Village Fun Day. *Literal AF2*
b. The village has held a three-legged race before because they are trying to break a village record that has been set during a previous race. *Inference AF3*
c. The organisers are not trying to break the Guinness World Record because 551 pairs broke this record, which is more people than live in the village. *Deduction AF3*
d. The phrase 'get ready for a good time!' is used to persuade people to enter the race. *Inference AF5*

GO FOR GOLD!

a. 551 pairs of runners took part in the largest three-legged race in the world. *Literal AF2*
b. There is no age limit, to encourage as many people as possible to take part. *Inference AF3*
c. 'All ages will be catered for' means there will be something for everyone, no matter how old or young they are. *Deduction AF3, AF5*
d. Two purposes of the flier are to promote the Village Fun Day; to encourage people to enter the three-legged race. *Deduction AF6*

BEYOND THE RECORD

Imagine you are organising a School Fun Day. What sort of activities and events will you have? Write five questions for a questionnaire to find out which activities would be the most popular with the children in your class.

Background research, reading and discussion to help the children to prepare

- Split the children into small groups and ask them to discuss the types of events, activities and stalls they would like to have at a School Fun Day.
- Bring the class back together and ask each group in turn to share their ideas. Draw up a shared list on the whiteboard.
- Discuss the format of questions that the children should include in their questionnaire, e.g. multiple choice, tick boxes, space to write answers or to rank choices.
- What else will the children need to include in their questionnaire? An introductory paragraph explaining how the information will be used, a line of thanks at the bottom?

Recording their ideas

- How will children decide on the wording of their questions? Will they draft them first and then ask for feedback from other children?
- How will children record their questions? On paper, using a word-processing tool, within a Microsoft PowerPoint® presentation with some level of interactivity for the user?

LANGUAGE ACTIVITY WORKSHEET

- As a class, look at the bulleted list in the text and discuss how it is punctuated.
- Ask the children to create their own flier for a School Fun Day. They should choose five events from the list of attractions on the worksheet. Ask them to write their chosen five events as a bulleted list.
- The children should write a short paragraph to introduce the School Fun Day and end with one or two sentences to persuade people to attend.

NAME: 　　　　　　　　　　　　　　　　　　　　DATE:

PERSUADING PEOPLE

A persuasive text tries to make the reader think, do or buy something.

Imagine you are designing a flier for a School Fun Day.

Write an opening paragraph, then choose events that you want to include from the suggestions below.

Write the events in a bulleted list and then write one or two sentences at the bottom of the flier to persuade people to attend.

three-legged race　　**skittles**　　**obstacle race**　　**book stall**　　**toy stall**　　**jungle gym**
bouncy castle　　**food and drink stall**　　**storyteller tent**　　**wet-sponge stocks**
micro-scooter course　　**folk dancers**

SCHOOL FUN DAY

GUINNESS WORLD RECORDS

RECORD-BREAKING COMPREHENSION – YEAR 5

LONGEST CAREER AS A WEATHER FORECASTER

This web page describes the importance of accurate weather forecasts and highlights the career of Dave Devall, who earned the Guinness World Record for the longest career as a weather forecaster.

Text type:	explanation/recount
AFs covered:	AF2, AF3, AF5
Specialist vocabulary:	weather, forecast, reliable, livestock, hurricane, barbecue, popular

ON YOUR MARKS

a. The worst storm in living memory struck Britain in 1987. *Literal AF2*
b. Weather forecasts are important for sailors because wind speed and wind direction affect conditions at sea and therefore how and where sailors sail. *Deduction AF3*
c. 2009 wasn't a 'barbecue summer' because it rained and was cold; not suitable weather for having a barbecue. *Deduction AF3*
d. Weather forecasters sometimes make mistakes because the weather conditions can change very quickly. *Inference AF3*

GET SET

a. The south of Britain was hit by the 1987 storm. *Literal AF2*
b. The weather forecast helps farmers by letting them know when they should harvest crops (during fine weather) or bring livestock inside (when wet weather is forecast). *Deduction AF3*
c. The weather forecaster from 1987 hasn't been allowed to forget his mistake because people weren't prepared for the storm and suffered as a result. *Inference AF3*
d. The word 'reliable' means something that can be trusted. *Deduction AF3, AF5*

GO FOR GOLD!

a. Dave Devall was a TV weather forecaster in Ontario. *Literal AF2*
b. Forecasters are unpopular when they forecast fine weather that doesn't come. *Deduction AF3*
c. The word 'not' is in italics to give it extra emphasis. *Deduction AF5*
d. Dave Devall 'can't have got it wrong too often' because his career as a weather forecaster lasted for over 48 years. *Inference AF3*

BEYOND THE RECORD

Watch one weather forecast every day for a week and write down what the weather is like each day. At the end of the week, compare each forecast with the actual weather for that day. How accurate were each of the weather forecasts?

Background research, reading and discussion to help the children to prepare

- If possible, introduce the activity by looking at online weather forecasts such as www.bbc.co.uk/weather/.
- Discuss the key information that children should note down, such as temperature, rainfall and wind speed.
- Discuss the accuracy of short- and long-term weather forecasts.

Recording their ideas

- How will the children record their ideas? Will they keep a record electronically or create a handwritten summary with consistent headings for each day? Will they use illustrations to depict weather types, or give written descriptions?
- Will children record the weather predictions for their local area only? Could they share weather observations with another school in a different part of the UK?

LANGUAGE ACTIVITY WORKSHEET

- Discuss with the children any words and phrases relating to the weather that they have learned by watching weather forecasts. Write their suggestions on the whiteboard.
- Explain to the children that a dictionary can be used not only to check spellings of words but also to find out the meaning, or definition, of words.
- Ask children to use a hard-copy, or online, dictionary to find the definition of each of the weather-related words on the worksheet.
- Fast finishers can add their own weather-related word and an appropriate definition.

NAME: DATE:

DESCRIBING THE WEATHER
We can use a dictionary to check spellings and definitions of words.

Use a dictionary to find the definition of each of these weather-related words. Write your own weather-related word, with its definition, in the blank box.

- squally
- isobar
- precipitation
- meteorology
- barometer
- atmosphere

GUINNESS WORLD RECORDS

RECORD-BREAKING COMPREHENSION – YEAR 5

LARGEST BHANGRA DANCE

This diary entry, written from the perspective of a child visiting her family in India, recounts a trip to see the Guinness World Record attempt for the largest bhangra dance, which was performed in India in 2010.

Text type:	recount
AFs covered:	AF2, AF3, AF5, AF6, AF7
Specialist vocabulary:	bhangra, lecturer, agricultural, university, initially, atmosphere, foundation, achieved, experience

ON YOUR MARKS

a. The author was staying with her aunty and uncle. *Literal AF2*
b. The author thought the dancing was fabulous. *Inference AF3*
c. Her uncle worked as a lecturer at the university where the record attempt was held. *Deduction AF3*
d. The author begged her uncle to take her because she loves bhangra. *Deduction AF3*

GET SET

a. The Art of Living Foundation organised the record attempt. *Literal AF2*
b. When she wrote 'The atmosphere was electric!', she meant that everyone at the record attempt was very excited. *Inference AF5, AF6*
c. Before the dancing started, the author was uninterested in what was going on because someone was giving a speech. *Deduction AF3*
d. The author said it was 'fabulous for everybody' because the dancers and audience had come to the event hoping that the record would be broken. *Deduction AF3*

GO FOR GOLD!

a. The two adjectives the author uses are 'crowded' and 'hot'. *Literal AF2*
b. The following words and phrases show this is an informal recount: 'I love bhangra!'; 'so much fun'; 'surprise of my life'; 'I cannot believe my luck'; 'I begged him to take me'; 'unbelievably'; 'I wasn't too bothered' (any two of these answers are acceptable). *Deduction AF5, AF6*
c. At first the author was excited to be there, then disappointed because she couldn't see much, then excited again when she stood on her chair and could see everything. *Inference AF3*
d. This text is similar to other recounts in that it describes an event that has already happened, uses the first person and past-tense verbs. *Deduction AF7*

BEYOND THE RECORD

Bhangra is a type of folk dance from India. Use the internet to find out about other kinds of traditional dance from five countries around the world.

Background research, reading and discussion to help the children to prepare

- Look at websites such as www.fitforafeast.com/dance_cultural.htm (You may want to choose a selection of suitable dances in advance.) With the children, draw up a list of up to 10 dances.
- The children should use a safe internet search to find out more information about their favourite five dances.

Recording their ideas

- How will the children present their information, e.g. as an alphabetical guide, paragraphs with sub-headings?
- Will the children use video stills or photos of the dances? (Ensure they acknowledge the source of the images if they choose to do this.)

LANGUAGE ACTIVITY WORKSHEET

- This worksheet can be used to revise the use of suffixes.
- Ask the children to list any adjectives they know with the *–able* or *–ible* endings.
- The *–able* words are formed by adding the suffix onto a verb, e.g. *comfort + able*. The *–ible* suffix is added to words of Latin origin. The children will need to think of a related root word, e.g. *visible* is related to *vision*, and then work out the phrase, e.g. *vision* means able to be seen. Dictionaries may be helpful during this exercise.
- Fast finishers can move on to writing a rule for when to use each suffix.

Answers: comfort/to comfort; predict/to predict; bend/to bend; believe/to believe; see/to see; eat/to eat. Rule: the *–able* suffix should be used only with verbs that are complete. The *–ible* suffix should be used for verb phrases.

NAME: _____   DATE: _____

THE SUFFIX DANCE

The suffixes *-ible* and *-able* are used to change a verb into an adjective.

Write the verbs or verb phrases that relate to these adjectives.

1. Comfortable _____

2. Predictable _____

3. Bendable _____

4. Credible _____

5. Visible _____

6. Edible _____

Choose one of the adjectives above and use it in a sentence.

_____
_____
_____
_____

Do you know when to use the suffix *-ible* and when to use the suffix *-able*? Work out a rule to help you remember when to use each suffix.

_____
_____
_____
_____

© Rising Stars UK Ltd. 2013   Record-Breaking Comprehension/Year 5/Largest bhangra dance

GUINNESS WORLD RECORDS

RECORD-BREAKING COMPREHENSION – YEAR 5

MOST GUIDE DOGS TRAINED BY AN ORGANISATION

This flier is written to persuade the reader to become a Puppy Walker for the Guide Dogs for the Blind Association (GDBA). The GDBA hold the Guinness World Record for the most guide dogs trained by an organisation.

Text type:	persuasion
AFs covered:	AF2, AF3, AF4, AF5, AF6
Specialist vocabulary:	volunteer, commitment, partially, familiarise, supervisor, process, community, association

ON YOUR MARKS

a. The Guide Dogs for the Blind Association trains dogs to provide mobility assistance to blind and partially sighted people. *Literal AF2*

b. A Puppy Walker would need lots of time, commitment and love because young puppies are demanding and need to be trained to be calm and well behaved. *Deduction AF3*

c. This is a persuasive text. *Deduction AF4*

d. The phrase 'thrown in at the deep end' literally means throwing someone in at the deep end of a swimming pool before they can swim. In the flier, the phrase means making someone do something difficult without preparing them for it or providing help. *Inference AF5*

GET SET

a. A puppy is kept from six weeks until it is one year old. *Literal AF2*

b. The author is trying to get the reader to become a Puppy Walker. *Deduction AF6*

c. Puppy Walkers play a vital role because they help to train the puppies, and as volunteers they don't cost the charity any money. *Inference AF3*

d. The text says 'You could make a difference' to make you feel that the job is special and to want to volunteer. *Inference AF5, AF6*

GO FOR GOLD!

a. Puppy Walkers are supported by GDBA Puppy Walker Supervisors. *Literal AF2*

b. The rewards of being a Puppy Walker are: seeing a puppy grow up and learn new skills; making new friends and knowing you have been useful to a blind or partially sighted person. *Deduction AF3*

c. 'Mobility assistance' means helping someone move around. *Deduction AF3, AF5*

d. The text asks the reader questions to make the reader think about the answers they would give. *Inference AF6*

BEYOND THE RECORD

What do you think the best and worst aspects of being a Puppy Walker might be? Write a balanced argument giving the pros and cons.

Background research, reading and discussion to help the children to prepare

- Read through the text as a class. Discuss with the children the good and bad things about being a Puppy Walker.
- Draw up a chart with a 'pro' column and a 'con' column and write in the children's ideas and suggestions. Children should refer to this when writing their balanced argument.

Recording their ideas

- How will the children structure their balanced argument? All pros and all cons grouped together, one pro offset by one con?
- Will they create a handwritten draft and then write this up neatly, or use a computer or tablet to type their argument and then edit it afterwards?

Ideas: pros: meet new people, opportunity to help others through volunteering, learn more about training a dog, get more exercise; cons: takes up a lot of time, would need to pay for dog food and bedding, have to return the dog.

LANGUAGE ACTIVITY WORKSHEET

- Use this worksheet to look at relative clauses.
- Explain that we use relative clauses to give more information about a subject without having to start another sentence. These clauses usually begin with *who, where, why, which, whose* and *that*.
- Explain that a word is missing from each of the sentences on the worksheet, at the beginning of the relative clause. Ask the children to choose a word from the word box to complete the sentences so they make sense.
- When they have written the word in the sentence, ask the children to read it aloud to check for sense.

Answers: whose, which, where, who, which.

NAME: DATE:

RELATIVE CLAUSES

A relative clause makes the meaning of a noun more specific. For example:

That's the <u>dog</u> <u>who lives with our neighbour</u>.

noun   relative clause

A word is missing from the beginning of the clauses in these sentences. Choose the best word from the word box to make sense of each of the sentences.

1. The Puppy Walker, _____ puppy is the best behaved, gets a prize.

2. I volunteered to be a Puppy Walker, _____ takes up a lot of time!

3. Look in the corner _____ the puppy's toys are kept.

4. The puppy _____ makes the most progress will get a reward.

5. My puppy wouldn't walk on the lead, _____ was a real problem.

Word box: who, where, whose, which

Write two of your own sentences using a relative clause.

1. _____

_____

2. _____

_____

© Rising Stars UK Ltd. 2013   Record-Breaking Comprehension/Year 5/Most guide dogs trained by an organisation

GUINNESS WORLD RECORDS

RECORD-BREAKING COMPREHENSION – YEAR 5

FARTHEST DISTANCE LIMBO-SKATING UNDER CARS

This text, in the form of a newspaper article, recounts how Rohan Kokane limbo-skated under a line of cars to achieve a Guinness World Record. It is laid out as a typical newspaper with a headline, lead sentence and text in columns.

Text type:	recount
AFs covered:	AF2, AF3, AF4, AF5
Specialist vocabulary:	gliding, aerodrome, lycra, parallel, emerged, flexible, controlled

ANSWERS

ON YOUR MARKS

a. Rohan achieved the Guinness World Record on Thursday, 17 February 2011. *Literal AF2*
b. Rohan set off some distance away from the cars so he could build up speed. *Deduction AF3*
c. The headline, name of the newspaper, date, introductory sentence and text laid out in columns tell us this is a newspaper article. *Deduction AF4*
d. *Personal opinion AF3*

GET SET

a. Rohan limbo-skated 38.68 m. *Literal AF2*
b. Rohan needed to build up speed so that he could glide for a long distance. *Deduction AF3*
c. Rohan jumped for joy because he was so pleased he had succeeded in achieving the Guinness World Record. *Inference AF3*
d. You need to be flexible to limbo-skate so that you can make your body go as low as possible. *Deduction AF3*

GO FOR GOLD!

a. The gap under the line of cars was 35 cm. *Literal AF2*
b. Rohan stays flexible by practising for four hours a day. *Literal AF3*
c. 'Emerged' means to move out or away from something and come into view. *Deduction AF5*
d. *Personal opinion AF3*

BEYOND THE RECORD

Imagine you are a television news reporter covering the record attempt. Write a short script for your broadcast, using the information in the newspaper report. What powerful adjectives will you use to keep your viewers interested?

Background research, reading and discussion to help the children to prepare

- Ask the children to suggest how a TV commentary on the record attempt as it took place would differ from a newspaper recount, e.g. use of present tense, conversational tone mixed with background information.
- As a class, create a list of powerful adjectives that the children can refer to when writing their script.

Recording their ideas

- How will the children note down the key information about the record attempt? Highlight information in the reading comprehension text, make handwritten notes in the margin, type up their ideas using a computer or tablet?
- How will the children record emphasis in their script? Italics, emboldening, exclamation marks, instructions in square brackets?

Feedback: Encourage the children to role-play their commentaries with a partner, sharing feedback so that the scripts can be improved.

LANGUAGE ACTIVITY WORKSHEET

- This worksheet can be used to revise and practise the use of suffixes.
- Ask the children to find the word *controlled* in the reading comprehension text. Ask them to identify the root word: *control*.
- Using the examples at the top of the worksheet, explain that the consonant is doubled when adding a vowel suffix to a word ending with a vowel and *l*. When the word has a pair of vowels followed by *l*, only the suffix is added.
- Provide the children with the worksheet and ask them to add the suffix *-ed* to the words. Fast finishers can write down four more verbs and add the suffix.

Answers: travelled, parcelled, revealed, fulfilled, foiled, rivalled, oiled, gravelled.

NAME: DATE:

–ED ENDINGS

When a word ends in a single vowel and the letter *l*, you double the *l* before adding a vowel suffix.

control + ed = controlled

When a word ends in two vowels and the letter *l*, you just add the suffix.

wheel + ed = wheeled

Add the suffix *-ed* to these verbs.

1. travel _____

2. parcel _____

3. reveal _____

4. fulfil _____

5. foil _____

6. rival _____

7. oil _____

8. gravel _____

Write down four more verbs ending in *l* and add the suffix *–ed*.

1. _____ + -ed = _____

2. _____ + -ed = _____

3. _____ + -ed = _____

4. _____ + -ed = _____

© Rising Stars UK Ltd. 2013   Record-Breaking Comprehension/Year 5/Farthest distance limbo-skating under cars

GUINNESS WORLD RECORDS

RECORD-BREAKING COMPREHENSION – YEAR 5

YOUNGEST MALE TO ROW AN OCEAN SOLO

This text describes Oliver Hicks' record-breaking solo row across the Atlantic Ocean. It also explains the dangers faced by sailors attempting to cross the Atlantic alone.

Text type:	recount/non-chronological report
AFs covered:	AF2, AF3, AF5, AF6
Specialist vocabulary:	container, submerged, pressure, generate, gigantic, freighter, hurricane

ON YOUR MARKS

a. The chance of being rescued is very slim. *Literal AF2*
b. The crew on a freighter might not spot a rowing boat because rowing boats are very small and therefore hard to see in the dark. *Deduction AF3*
c. 'Rowing solo' means rowing alone. *Deduction AF3, AF5*
d. A freak wave might be dangerous because it could easily overturn a rowing boat. *Inference AF3*

GET SET

a. A whale could cause a swell that swamps the boat, or dive underneath the boat and overturn it. *Literal AF2*
b. The purpose of this text is to show how brave Oliver Hicks was, by listing the dangers of rowing solo across an ocean. *Deduction AF6*
c. It is difficult to judge the distance of a boat at night because it is dark and there are no landmarks to help you. *Inference AF3*
d. If you hit a plastic container, it might break an oar or make a hole in the boat. *Inference AF3*

GO FOR GOLD!

a. An underwater volcanic eruption can generate gigantic waves. *Literal AF2*
b. The word 'hazard' means danger. *Deduction AF5*
c. Waves could swamp the boat or overturn it. *Deduction AF3*
d. Personal opinion *AF3*

BEYOND THE RECORD

What equipment do you think would be essential for a journey like this? Write a kit list for a long-distance rowing journey.

Background research, reading and discussion to help the children to prepare

- Remind the children how long Oliver Hicks was at sea (123 days, 22 hours, 8 minutes).
- Split children into groups and ask them to discuss what they would need to take with them on such a long journey. Encourage them to think of the problems they might encounter on the journey and how they could prepare for these. Remind them that only essential kit should be included.
- Bring the class back together and ask each group to share their ideas. List their suggestions on the board.

Recording their ideas

- How will the children record their kit list? As a handwritten document, typed up on the computer, recorded as a sound or video clip?
- How detailed will the list be? Will children provide information about the number of each item required (for example, the number of meals, volume of water, number of different items of clothing)?

Ideas: food, water, waterproof clothes, radio, GPS device, life jacket, first-aid kit, stove, emergency flare.

LANGUAGE ACTIVITY WORKSHEET

- Explain to the children that they can fillet (or précis) a passage to identify the key pieces of information by crossing out what is not essential.
- Ask the children to go through the text and cross out anything that can be omitted without losing the key information.
- Ask them to read the précised passage to a partner and check that it still gives the key points while retaining the sense of the original passage. Give them the opportunity to make adjustments if they need to. They can then count the number of words left.

NAME: DATE:

PRÉCIS

Sometimes we need to delete words to make a text shorter, but it is important to keep all the key information.

Cross out words in this text to make it as short as possible. Make sure you don't delete any key information.

Crossing any ocean or sea in a ship is usually very safe. Crossing the Atlantic Ocean alone in a rowing boat, without any support, is a very dangerous activity.

FLOATING CONTAINERS
Half-submerged plastic containers are a hazard if you hit them.

FALLING OVERBOARD
If you are rowing solo on the ocean and fall overboard, the chance of being rescued is very slim.

WHALES
Whales can be very dangerous if they swim too close to a small boat. They can cause a swell that swamps the boat, or dive underwater and upturn the boat.

FREAK WAVES
Pressure waves from underwater volcanic eruptions can generate gigantic waves in an otherwise calm sea.

FREIGHTERS
It is difficult to judge the distance of a boat at night. You can be hit by a freighter because the crew on board have not spotted your craft.

WEATHER
You might encounter storms or even hurricanes. The waves in the Atlantic Ocean can be huge.

Does the text still make sense?

GUINNESS WORLD RECORDS

RECORD-BREAKING COMPREHENSION – YEAR 5

HOTTEST CHILLI

This page from a gardening book provides step-by-step instructions on how to grow chillies. A fact box about hot chillies includes details of the Trinidad Scorpion 'Butch T' chilli, which holds the Guinness World Record for the hottest chilli in the world.

Text type:	instructions/non-chronological report
AFs covered:	AF2, AF3, AF4, AF5, AF7
Specialist vocabulary:	Habanero, airing, transplant, bushiness, Scoville, cayenne

ANSWERS

ON YOUR MARKS

a. You should plant the chilli seeds 5 cm apart. *Literal AF2*
b. You should water the seeds 'gently' so you don't wash them away. *Deduction AF3, AF5*
c. You should let the chillies turn red so they become hotter. *Deduction AF3*
d. You should feed the plants with tomato food to help them grow bigger. *Inference AF3*

GET SET

a. When the seedlings appear, you should move the tray to a warm, light place. *Literal AF2*
b. To stop the compost drying out, you should water regularly. *Deduction AF3*
c. The 'Can you take the heat?' sub-heading is used to draw attention to the information about very hot chillies. *Inference AF5*
d. The order is important because the steps need to be carried out in a particular sequence or the process will not make sense. *Deduction AF4*

GO FOR GOLD!

a. You should snip off the first chillies to encourage more to grow. *Literal AF2*
b. The seed tray should be covered with cling film to keep the moisture in and the soil warm. *Inference AF3*
c. The world's hottest chilli is 1,413,700 Scoville Heat Units hotter than cayenne pepper, which itself is quite hot. *Deduction AF3*
d. *Personal opinion AF7*

BEYOND THE RECORD

Chillies are used in cooking to make food taste spicy or hot. Find 10 recipes that contain chillies and create a chart to grade the spiciness of each recipe.

Background research, reading and discussion to help the children to prepare

- Ask the children if they have ever eaten food with chillies in, or know of any spicy dishes. Make a list of these dishes on the board.
- Provide them with a selection of recipe books or ask them to use the internet to find 10 recipes that contain chillies (if children are searching the internet independently ensure that safety measures are in place).

Recording their ideas

- How will children rate the spiciness of each recipe? Will they count the relative number of chillies used per portion, or use a rating system already used in the recipe book or website?
- How will the children structure their chart? Will they use symbols, numbers or words to grade the spiciness of each recipe?

LANGUAGE ACTIVITY WORKSHEET

- Use this worksheet to revise work on homophones.
- Explain that there are many homophones in English – words that sound the same but mean something different. Ask the children if they can think of any words that sound the same as *chilli* but mean something else.
- The worksheet lists eight food-related words with their definitions and, for each one, there is also the definition of a homophone.
- Ask the children to read the definition and write the homophone. They should check their spelling using a dictionary.

Answers: chilly, bury, place, doe, leaves, bred, serial.

NAME: DATE:

SAME SOUND, DIFFERENT MEANING

Homophones are words that sound the same but have different meanings.

Eight food-related words are listed below, with their definitions. A definition for a homophone is provided for each word, in the right-hand column. Read the definition and write the homophone in the space provided.

Take care with spellings.

chilli:
a spice

_____:
feeling cold

berry:
fruit from a plant

_____:
put into the ground

plaice:
a type of white fish

_____:
to put

dough:
uncooked bread

_____:
a female deer

leaves:
part of a salad

_____:
goes away

bread:
baked in an oven

_____:
past tense of breed

cereal:
seeds such as wheat

_____:
a story told in episodes

_____

© Rising Stars UK Ltd. 2013   Record-Breaking Comprehension/Year 5/Hottest chilli

GUINNESS WORLD RECORDS

RECORD-BREAKING COMPREHENSION – YEAR 5

MOST SKATEBOARD NOLLIES IN 30 SECONDS

This text describes popular skateboarding tricks and instructions for how to perform them. It includes information about the Guinness World Record for the most skateboard nollies in 30 seconds and is written in the style of a Sunday supplement section for children.

Text type:	instructions
AFs covered:	AF2, AF3, AF4, AF5, AF7
Specialist vocabulary:	skateboarding, basis, variation, achieved, impressive

ANSWERS

ON YOUR MARKS

a. The name of the trick in which you jump over a rail is the hippy jump. *Literal AF2*
b. The phrase 'hooked on' literally means to be caught or trapped on an object. In this text the phrase means being so 'caught up' in skateboarding that you want to keep on doing it. *Deduction AF3, AF5*
c. Practising would help you land more tricks because it helps you get better at the skateboarding tricks. *Inference AF3*
d. The easiest trick is the hippy jump because the board stays on the ground. *Inference, personal opinion AF3*

GET SET

a. The record for the most nollies in 30 seconds is 15. *Literal AF2*
b. On average, it took Ivan Sebastian Cordova two seconds to do a single nollie. *Deduction AF3*
c. Safety information is highlighted by a hazard symbol. *Deduction AF4, AF3*
d. The pop shove is the most difficult trick because you need to make the board spin. *Inference, personal opinion AF3*

GO FOR GOLD!

a. In a nollie, you flick up the nose of the board instead of the back. *Literal AF2*
b. The name 'nollie' comes from combining 'nose' and 'ollie'. *Deduction AF3, AF5*
c. The author has written the instructional text in the present tense because the actions being performed are happening in the present. *Deduction AF7*
d. When trying a new trick you might fall off the skateboard and injure yourself. *Inference, personal opinion AF3*

BEYOND THE RECORD

Find out more about one of the tricks in the text. Use this information to write a short script for the presenter of a skateboarding 'how to' video.

Background research, reading and discussion to help the children to prepare

- Discuss the format of any 'how to' videos the children have seen, e.g. on the internet or on TV. What kind of language is used? How is the 'how to' video structured?
- Visit www.howtoskatevideos.com/ for a selection of skateboarding 'how to' videos. Alternatively, search on YouTube for a suitable video. Select a clip to share with the class.
- Guide the children to websites to find out more about their chosen trick, e.g. www.how2skate.com/tricktips.htm, www.skateboardhere.com/skateboard-tricks.html.

Recording their ideas

- Ask children to think about the best way of recording information: facts written on sticky notes, notes written on paper under sub-headings, sentences typed into a word-processing tool?
- How will the children structure their information? How will they make the steps clear? Using time connectives, or numbering each step?

Feedback: Encourage the children to read out their scripts to others in the class. Are the instructions clear? Is any vital information missing?

LANGUAGE ACTIVITY WORKSHEET

- Use this worksheet to revise nouns and verbs that are commonly confused and to allow children to practise using these words in context.
- Ask the children to find the word *practise* in the text. Ask them if this is a noun or a verb.
- Explain that there are several words for which the noun and verb sound exactly, or nearly, the same but have different spellings. The former are called homophones. Explain the rule that the *ice* ending is used for a noun and the *ise* ending is used for a verb.

Answers: practise (verb), practice (noun): homophones; advise (verb), advice (noun): not homophones; devise (verb), device (noun): not homophones.

NAME: DATE:

PRACTISE, PRACTISE, PRACTISE

OFFICIALLY AMAZING

Homophones are words that sound the same but have different meanings. There are other pairs of words that are not true homophones: they sound similar and have different meanings.

The words below are a mixture of verbs and nouns. For each word, circle 'noun' or 'verb'. Then draw a tick or a cross to indicate whether the pairs are true homophones.

Finally, write a sentence about skateboarding using each of the words.

practise   noun/verb

practice   noun/verb

☐ Homophones?

_____
_____

advise   noun/verb

advice   noun/verb

☐ Homophones?

_____
_____

devise   noun/verb

device   noun/verb

☐ Homophones?

_____
_____

© Rising Stars UK Ltd. 2013   Record-Breaking Comprehension/Year 5/Most skateboard nollies in 30 seconds

GUINNESS WORLD RECORDS

RECORD-BREAKING COMPREHENSION – YEAR 5

LARGEST HANDS

This text contains information about how bacteria are spread and gives instructions on how to wash your hands properly. It is based on the Guinness World Record for the largest hands.

Text type:	instructions /non-chronological report
AFs covered:	AF2, AF3, AF6, AF7
Specialist vocabulary:	bacteria, transferring, bacterial, infection, hygienic

ON YOUR MARKS

a. The most common way bacteria are spread is by not washing your hands properly (or at all!). *Literal AF2*
b. You should rub in between all your fingers to remove any bacteria there. *Inference AF3*
c. You should wash your hands after handling an animal because it might have transferred bacteria to your hands. *Inference AF3*
d. Sultan Kösen must feel pleased/proud about having the largest hands because it makes him exceptional/gained him the Guinness World Record. *Personal opinion, inference AF3*

GET SET

a. It should take at least 15 seconds to wash your hands. *Literal AF2*
b. If you didn't wash your hands before touching a cut or graze, it might get infected. *Inference AF3*
c. A hand-drier machine is more hygienic than using a towel because bacteria might be found on a towel. *Inference AF3*
d. It is important to dry your hands thoroughly to avoid the spread of bacteria. *Deduction AF3*

GO FOR GOLD!

a. Sultan Kösen's hands are 28.5 cm long. *Literal AF2*
b. Washing your hands helps stop the spread of bacteria because it stops you transferring bacteria from your own hands onto things that other people touch. *Deduction AF3*
c. The main purpose of the poster is to remind people how to stop the spread of bacteria and illness by washing their hands properly. *Inference AF6*
d. Personal opinion *AF7*

BEYOND THE RECORD

Use a computer to create a poster that encourages children in your school to wash their hands thoroughly. Search the internet for some key facts about hand washing and choose which facts to use on your poster.

Background research, reading and discussion to help the children to prepare

- Make sure children have access to the reading comprehension text. Guide them to sites such as www.wash-hands.com/ to find out more information.
- Talk about the audience for their posters. What sort of design features and language might be attractive to this age group?

Recording their ideas

- How will children select the most important information for their poster? Highlight key information, make brief handwritten notes, or type directly into a word-processing tool for later editing?
- What organisational features will the children use in this poster? Bulleted or numbered lists, fact boxes, images with captions, clear headings? Will they use colour?

LANGUAGE ACTIVITY WORKSHEET

- Use this worksheet to revise the use of bulleted lists in texts and reordering sequences of instructions.
- Ask the children to suggest how they should capitalise and punctuate a bulleted list. Encourage them to check their ideas against the bullet points in the text.
- Provide the children with the worksheet and ask them to rewrite each step in the correct order as a bulleted list, using the correct punctuation.
- Fast finishers should move on to creating their own, correctly punctuated, sequence of instructions.

Answers: To wash your hair properly, you should: rinse with warm water/add shampoo/lather shampoo all over your hair/rinse with warm water/repeat the last three steps.

NAME: DATE:

BULLET POINTS

Bullet points are used to list important information. Bulleted lists should not be too long and should be consistent in design (dots, dashes, squares) and layout, e.g. all capitals or no capitals at the beginning of each bullet point, but not a mix.

The text below is in the wrong order and has not been punctuated or capitalised consistently. Write the text as a bulleted list, using consistent punctuation and capitalisation.

to wash your hair properly you should

Add shampoo

rinse with warm water

Repeat the last three steps

Rinse with warm water

lather shampoo all over your hair

_____

- _____

- _____

- _____

- _____

- _____

Now write your own bulleted list for a different process that you do every day, such as brushing your teeth.

To _____ , you should:

- _____

- _____

- _____

- _____

- _____

GUINNESS WORLD RECORDS

RECORD-BREAKING COMPREHENSION – YEAR 5

FASTEST TALKER

This page from a children's educational website gives information about the speed at which people talk. It also features details of the Guinness World Record for the fastest talker in the English language.

Text type:	non-chronological report
AFs covered:	AF2, AF3, AF4, AF5
Specialist vocabulary:	language, Sanskrit, Sumerian, Hebrew, Basque, foreign, syllable, recited, soliloquy, blatteroon

ON YOUR MARKS

a. Over 7,000 different languages are spoken in the world today. *Literal AF2*
b. Bullet points are used to make the information stand out from the rest of the text. *Deduction AF4*
c. 'Blending' means mixing together. *Deduction AF3, AF5*
d. Apart from talking, people can communicate with each other by writing, hand signals and body language. *Deduction, personal opinion AF3*

GET SET

a. Some of the oldest languages in the world are Sanskrit, Sumerian, Hebrew and Basque (any two of these answers are acceptable). *Literal AF2*
b. The verb 'recited' means to learn something by heart and speak it out loud. *Deduction AF3, AF5*
c. The author starts the main text with a question to draw the reader into the text. *Inference AF3*
d. *Personal opinion AF3*

GO FOR GOLD!

a. The fastest spoken language is Japanese. *Literal AF2*
b. A soliloquy is a speech in which a character talks to him or herself. *Deduction AF5*
c. A fast talker could trick or mislead people by talking very quickly to persuade them to do something that they may not want to do. *Inference, personal opinion AF5*
d. The same soliloquy is always used for this record attempt so that the challenge is the same for everyone and no one has an unfair advantage when the attempt is measured. *Inference AF3*

BEYOND THE RECORD

How fast can you read out loud? Time yourself reading the first three lines of Hamlet's 'To be or not to be' soliloquy. Count the syllables in the text and work out how many syllables you read per second. Ask a partner to read the same text. Time them and see who is the fastest reader.

Background research, reading and discussion to help the children to prepare

- Provide the children with copies of Hamlet's 'To be or not to be' soliloquy. See http://en.wikipedia.org/wiki/To_be,_or_not_to_be.
- Will the children have more than one attempt? Discuss the effect that practising might have on their reading speed.
- Ensure the children are clear about how to work out their reading speed (divide the number of syllables by the number of seconds).

Recording their ideas

- How will the children record their speed reading? In a class table on the board or typed into a spreadsheet on the computer, where the results can be analysed further?

LANGUAGE ACTIVITY WORKSHEET

- This worksheet allows the children to practise proofreading a text. Provide the children with the worksheet and explain that 10 of the words have been misspelled. It is their task to proofread the text and underline the mistakes.
- The children should write out the correct spellings in the spelling box under the text. Encourage them to use a dictionary if they are unsure of a correct spelling. When the children have found and corrected the mistakes, they could self-mark or mark another child's work, using the text from the Pupil Book.

Answers: foreign, blending, carried, Japanese, syllables, language, soliloquy, approximately, measure, particular.

| NAME: | DATE: |

PROOFREADING FOR PUNCTUATION AND SPELLING

Proofreading your work can help you to correct spelling and punctuation errors.

There are 10 spelling mistakes in the text below. Proofread the text. Underline the wrong spellings and write the correct spellings in the box at the bottom of the page. Don't look at the original text until you have checked your work.

Did you know there are over 7,000 different languages spoken in the world today? The oldest of these languages are Sanskrit, Sumerian, Hebrew and Basque.

When you hear people talking in forein languages, what they are saying can often sound very fast, with words bleending into each other.

A study carryed out in France showed that the fastest spoken language is Japaneze, with an average of 7.84 sylables spoken each second!

The fastest talker in the English langage is Sean Shannon from Canada. He recited Hamlet's 260-word solliloquy 'To be or not to be' in 23.8 seconds in Edinburgh on 30 August 1995. That's approximatly 15 syllables per second. This soliloquy is always used to meashure speed talking for this partiqular Guinness World Record.

Correct spellings

1. _____
2. _____
3. _____
4. _____
5. _____
6. _____
7. _____
8. _____
9. _____
10. _____

GUINNESS WORLD RECORDS

RECORD-BREAKING COMPREHENSION – YEAR 5

TALLEST TEENAGER LIVING (MALE)

This explanation text explores the rate at which children of different ages grow. It includes information about Brenden Adams, who holds the Guinness World Record for the tallest teenager living (male).

Text type:	explanation
AFs covered:	AF2, AF3, AF4, AF5
Specialist vocabulary:	dependent, different, factor, height, growth, health, remarkable, spurt, scientist, adolescence, occurs, population, nutrition

ON YOUR MARKS

a. The average height for an adult male is 175 cm. *Literal AF2*
b. A 'growth spurt' is a lot of growth in a short period of time. *Deduction AF5*
c. A baby's growth rate slows down after the first year because if they kept growing at the same rate they would be the same size as an adult after only a few years. *Inference AF3*
d. *Personal opinion AF3*

GET SET

a. Children grow slightly faster during spring. *Literal AF2*
b. The sub-heading 'Height throughout history' uses alliteration. The author has done this to draw your attention to the information. *Deduction AF4, AF5*
c. The author uses the adjective 'healthy' because unhealthy babies might not grow as fast as healthy babies. *Deduction AF5*
d. *Personal opinion AF3*

GO FOR GOLD!

a. During adolescence a major growth spurt occurs. *Literal AF2*
b. If you have a poor diet, you might not get important nutrients your body needs to grow. *Deduction AF3*
c. The author uses the adjective 'remarkable' to show that 25 cm is a large amount to grow in a year. *Deduction AF5*
d. *Personal opinion AF3*

BEYOND THE RECORD

Use the information in the text to create an interesting PowerPoint® presentation about human growth. Share your presentation with your class and gather feedback. What could you do better next time?

Background research, reading and discussion to help the children to prepare

- As a class, agree on the audience for the PowerPoint® presentation, e.g. school children, parents, school governors.
- If appropriate, demonstrate how to add information to slides in PowerPoint® and any other tools or effects that children may wish to explore, such as setting slide transitions.

Recording their ideas

- How will the children select information from the text? Will they paraphrase ideas or use direct quotations?
- How will the children present the information on each slide? Will they consider font size and style, use of headings and bullets, colour and images?

Feedback: Encourage the children to share their presentations with the rest of the class and discuss what worked well and what could be improved.

LANGUAGE ACTIVITY WORKSHEET

- This worksheet can be used to revise work on punctuating sentences.
- Point to the example at the top of the worksheet. Explain that commas are used to punctuate the list, with a connective before the final list item.
- Ask the children to circle the connective used in each sentence and then to rewrite the sentences, using the correct punctuation.

Answers: Among the factors that affect your growth are your parents' height, your diet (and) your general health; I grew 1 cm, Joe grew 2 cm (but) Alisha grew 3 cm; Fruit, vegetables, water (and) protein make a healthy diet; Guy is average height, Harry is taller than average (and) Sandy is the tallest of all; Baby Faris has brown eyes, brown hair (and) soft skin; When he went shopping, he bought milk, pasta, cheese, tuna (and) eggs.

NAME: DATE:

PUNCTUATING LISTS

When lists of things are written in a sentence they are separated by commas, except for the final item, which is preceded by a simple connective.

We ate sandwiches, apples, bananas (and) yoghurts for our healthy lunch.

For each sentence below, circle the connective used. Then rewrite each sentence in the space provided and insert commas to punctuate the lists.

Among the factors that affect your growth are your parents' height your diet and your general health.

I grew 1 cm Joe grew 2 cm but Alisha grew 3 cm.

_____

_____

Fruit vegetables water and protein make a healthy diet.

_____

_____

Guy is average height Harry is taller than average and Sandy is the tallest of all.

_____

_____

Baby Faris has brown eyes brown hair and soft skin.

_____

_____

When he went shopping he bought milk pasta cheese tuna and eggs.

_____

_____

© Rising Stars UK Ltd. 2013   Record-Breaking Comprehension/Year 5/Tallest teenager living (male)

GUINNESS WORLD RECORDS

RECORD-BREAKING COMPREHENSION – YEAR 5

LARGEST VERTICAL GARDEN (GREEN WALL)

The text from this gardening book explains the benefits of vertical gardens and how they are created. The text also highlights the largest vertical garden (green wall), which is located at the Hotel Mercure Santo Domingo in Madrid, Spain.

Text type:	explanation/instructions
AFs covered:	AF2, AF3, AF5, AF6
Specialist vocabulary:	vertical, increase, complex, module, beneficial, natural, climber

ON YOUR MARKS

a. Green walls are useful for people with small gardens because they increase the planting area available. *Literal AF2*
b. Instructional text in the form of a bulleted list is provided in the box at the bottom left of the page. *Deduction AF3*
c. Green walls make a dull building or area look more attractive to passers-by. *Inference AF3*
d. *Personal opinion AF3*

GET SET

a. The simplest form of green wall consists of climbing plants growing up a wall. *Literal AF2*
b. You need to use 'natural climbers' because other plants would not climb upwards and cover the wall. *Deduction AF3*
c. The modules in complex green walls are filled with soil to provide something for the plant to grow in. *Inference AF3*
d. *Personal opinion AF6*

GO FOR GOLD!

a. Complex green walls are made by attaching special modules to a wall and filling them with soil and plants. *Literal AF2, AF3*
b. Plants should be tied to the frame or wire to keep them close to the wall and help them grow upwards. *Deduction AF3*
c. Green walls benefit wildlife by providing habitats for insects and birds. *Inference AF5*
d. *Personal opinion AF3*

BEYOND THE RECORD

Think of a place in your local area that could be made more attractive by planting a green wall. Write a persuasive letter to your local council, explaining why it should fund a green wall project.

Background reading and discussion to help the children to prepare
- Search online for images of green walls. Search terms might include: 'living walls', 'vertical planting systems', 'vertical gardens', 'plant walls' or 'vegetated walls'.
- Provide websites to investigate, e.g. www.hotelsantodomingo.es/en/hotel-mercure-santo-domingo.html.
- List the essentials, e.g. a larg(ish) empty wall, a frame to hold the soil and plants, etc.

Checklist for persuasive letter writing: layout, formal language, say why it is such a good idea, use catchy phrases to grab attention.

LANGUAGE ACTIVITY WORKSHEET

- Point out the word *beneficial* in the text. Discuss the prefix *bene-*, meaning *good*, and ask the children to say any words they already know that use this prefix (examples include 'benefit', 'benefactor', 'beneficiary', 'benevolent').

- The worksheet focuses on the common prefix *dis-* (which has negative connotations) and the less common prefix *im-*, meaning *not*. Children can use a dictionary (either printed or online).

- Ask the children to choose a word from each climber and use it in a sentence.

Possible answers: disagree, disappoint, disaster, disbelief, discomfort, discourage, discourteous, discriminate; impatient, impede, imperfect, impersonate, impossible, imposter, improper.

NAME: DATE:

PREFIX PLANTING

Beneficial uses the Latin prefix *bene-*, meaning *good*.

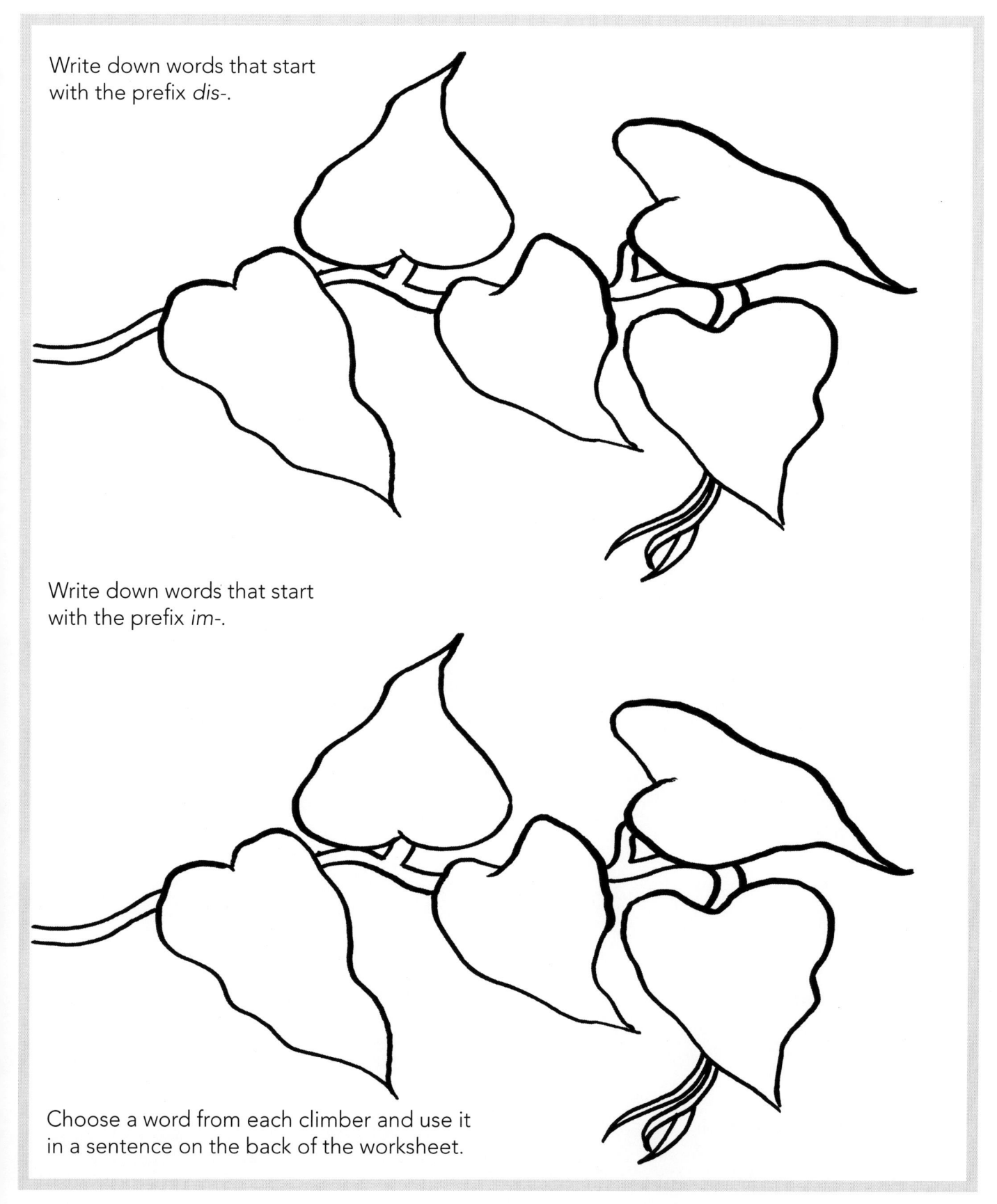

Write down words that start with the prefix *dis-*.

Write down words that start with the prefix *im-*.

Choose a word from each climber and use it in a sentence on the back of the worksheet.

© Rising Stars UK Ltd. 2013   Record-Breaking Comprehension/Year 5/Largest vertical garden (green wall)

GUINNESS WORLD RECORDS

RECORD-BREAKING COMPREHENSION – YEAR 5

LARGEST HAIRY FAMILY

This book page introduces the Gomez family, who hold the Guinness World Record for the largest hairy family. All members of the family have the rare medical condition Congenital Generalised Hypertrichosis, which causes the excessive growth of hair.

Text type:	explanation
AFs covered:	AF2, AF3, AF5
Specialist vocabulary:	Congenital Generalised, Hypertrichosis, excessive, werewolf, syndrome, national, trapeze, generation

ON YOUR MARKS

a. Danny and Larry started performing when they were six years old. *Literal AF2*
b. Congenital Generalised Hypertrichosis is known as 'Werewolf Syndrome' because the condition leads to the excessive growth of hair – something that happens when a werewolf changes from its human form into a wolf, according to myth and legend. *Inference AF3*
c. Danny and Larry Gomez call themselves 'The Wolf People' because they are covered in hair, like wolves, and it is a memorable stage name. *Deduction AF3*
d. Danny and Larry chose to become performers because this was a positive way to make the most of their hairy appearance. *Inference, personal opinion AF3*

GET SET

a. Danny and Larry Gomez perform in the Mexican National Circus. *Literal AF2*
b. 'Spans five generations' means that five generations of the family have had the condition. *Deduction AF5*
c. They use the names Danny and Larry because they are shorter than their own names and are easier for others to remember. *Deduction AF3*
d. Werewolves are imaginary. They do not exist and only appear in fictional stories. *Inference AF3*

GO FOR GOLD!

a. The hyphenated term is 'wolf-like'. *Literal AF2*
b. Members of the same family suffer from the condition because it is inherited. *Deduction AF3*
c. The adjective 'excessive' means more than is necessary. *Deduction AF3, AF5*
d. *Personal opinion AF3*

BEYOND THE RECORD

Imagine Danny and Larry are coming to visit your school. Write down a list of five questions you would like to ask them. With a partner, use your questions to role-play an interview with either Danny or Larry. When you have finished, swap roles and repeat the activity.

Background research, reading and discussion to help the children to prepare

- As a class, discuss the reading comprehension text and Danny and Larry Gomez. How do the children feel about the duo? What sorts of things would they like to know about them?
- Remind children of the need to ask open questions, rather than closed questions with yes or no answers.

Recording their ideas

- Either in pairs or small groups, encourage the children to brainstorm 10 or more questions.
- How will the children select their final five questions? Will they focus on questions about the backgrounds of the two performers? Or will their questions be mainly focused on their current life, including their performances? Encourage the children to consider whether the questions allow the duo to impart interesting views and information about themselves.

LANGUAGE ACTIVITY WORKSHEET

- Ask the children to find the term *duo* in the text.
- Explain that *duo* originates from Latin and that, in English, we often use Latin terms to describe groups of people who are involved in the performing arts.
- On the worksheet, ask the children to draw a line from each Latin word to its English equivalent. Encourage children to refer to a dictionary if they need to check meanings. Fast finishers should write a nonsense poem to help them remember the Latin meanings.

Answers: duo/two, trio/three, quartet/four, quintet/five, sextet/six, septet/seven, octet/eight.

NAME: DATE:

DUO OR TWO?

In English, we often use Latin terms to describe groups of people, especially in performing arts.

For example, *duo* means *two*.

Draw a line to match the Latin and English words.
One has been done as an example.

duo — three

trio — two

quartet   six

quintet   eight

sextet   four

septet   five

octet   seven

Write a nonsense poem to help you remember the meaning of each Latin word.

© Rising Stars UK Ltd. 2013   Record-Breaking Comprehension/Year 5/Largest hairy family

GUINNESS WORLD RECORDS

RECORD-BREAKING COMPREHENSION – YEAR 5

HEAVIEST VEHICLE PULLED BY HAIR (FEMALE)

This magazine text comprises a set of instructions for an experiment to test the strength of human hair and a recount of the Guinness World Record for the heaviest vehicle pulled by hair (female).

Text type:	instructions/recount
AFs covered:	AF2, AF3, AF4, AF5, AF7
Specialist vocabulary:	experiment, several, anchor, weight, vehicle

ON YOUR MARKS

a. You should hold the strand of hair near the root. *Literal AF2*
b. Bullet points are used to clearly list the equipment for the experiment and to separate the 'Did you know?' facts. *Deduction AF4*
c. You should count the number of pennies used when the strand of hair breaks to help you calculate the weight your hair can hold. *Deduction AF3*
d. You should anchor the pencil securely so it doesn't roll away or fall. *Deduction AF3*

GET SET

a. The weight of the vehicle was 8,835.5 kg. *Literal AF2*
b. The author asks a question and uses interesting language, such as 'hair-raising', to ensure the audience will keep reading. *Deduction AF5*
c. Rani used her whole head of hair because it is stronger than individual strands. *Inference AF3*
d. Rani probably prepared for the record attempt by practising pulling vehicles using her hair and using weights to make sure her muscles were strong. *Inference, personal opinion AF3*

GO FOR GOLD!

a. A head of human hair can support the weight of two elephants. *Literal AF2*
b. You should 'add more pennies one by one' so you know exactly how many pennies cause the hair to break. *Inference AF3*
c. The word 'gently' is in italics to emphasise how important it is to pull the hair out gently. *Deduction AF5*
d. *Personal opinion AF7*

BEYOND THE RECORD

Carry out experiments to find out the strength of other fine materials, such as cotton, cobwebs, plant fibres or grass. Use the numbered steps in the text to help you. Create a chart to show the results of your experiments.

Background research, reading and discussion to help the children to prepare

- Discuss what materials the children will test. Will they compare the strengths of two or more materials? What will they keep the same to make sure the test is fair (for example, the length of each material, the point where the weights are attached, etc.)?
- Talk about the weights to be used, for example pennies, counting cubes or individual gram weights.

Recording their ideas

- How will the children record their results? In a handwritten table on paper, or by inputting the results into an Excel spreadsheet on the computer?
- How will the children structure their table/chart? What headings will they use for each column?

LANGUAGE ACTIVITY WORKSHEET

- Explain to the children that the set of instructions from the text is given on the worksheet without the numbers for each step.
- Ask them to rewrite the instructions and sequence the steps with time-related connectives instead of numbers. Some connectives are provided to help, but explain that they can use other connectives if they wish to.
- Ask the children to read their instructions aloud and discuss how they are different from the numbered instructions. Ask them which they think works best.

Possible answers: First, Secondly, After that, Then, Next, Then, Finally.

NAME: DATE:

USING CONNECTIVES TO SEQUENCE INSTRUCTIONS

Connectives link different phrases, sentences and paragraphs.

GUINNESS WORLD RECORDS — OFFICIALLY AMAZING

Use time connectives to sequence these instructions. Rewrite the instructions on a separate piece of paper.

first   next   then   after that   later   now   secondly   finally

- Take a strand of your hair. Hold it near the root and pull it out gently.

- Tape the strand of hair to a pencil.

- Place a pile of books on top of the pencil to anchor it securely. The hair should hang downwards from the pencil.

- Carefully tape one penny to the end of the hair.

- Add more pennies, one by one.

- When the hair breaks, count the number of pennies taped to the hair.

- To work out the weight your hair can hold, multiply the number of pennies counted by 2.5 g.

On the back of this sheet, write a set of instructions for a different process, using time connectives.

© Rising Stars UK Ltd. 2013   Record-Breaking Comprehension/Year 5/Heaviest vehicle pulled by hair (female)

GUINNESS WORLD RECORDS

RECORD-BREAKING COMPREHENSION – YEAR 5

LARGEST GATHERING OF PEOPLE DRESSED AS LEPRECHAUNS

This text, based on the Guinness World Record for the largest gathering of people dressed as leprechauns, is a page from a guide to Ireland. It includes information about leprechauns, and a local legend.

Text type:	character sketch/legend
AFs covered:	AF2, AF3, AF5, AF6, AF7
Specialist vocabulary:	leprechaun, mischief, musician, whistle, secretive, creature, mischievously, desert, island

ON YOUR MARKS

a. Leprechauns wear green. *Literal AF2*
b. 'Mischievously' means in a naughty or troublesome way. *Deduction AF3, AF5*
c. The text says that leprechauns are secretive and rarely seen and so it would be very hard to find a leprechaun. But leprechauns are from Irish folklore and do not exist so it would be impossible to find one. *Deduction AF3*
d. Leprechauns are not dangerous. The text tells us that the tricks they play are generally harmless. *Inference AF3*

GET SET

a. The text says that leprechauns are rarely seen because they are secretive creatures and therefore hard to find. Leprechauns are fairy creatures from Irish folklore, so in reality they are rarely seen because they do not exist. *Literal, deduction AF2, AF3*
b. The author is proud of the Guinness World Record because he says 'our very own Ireland!' when describing it. *Deduction AF6*
c. Someone might regret catching a leprechaun because it would trick them and leave them worse off. *Deduction AF3*
d. *Personal opinion AF3*

GO FOR GOLD!

a. Someone might want to catch a leprechaun so they could take his pot of gold. *Literal AF2*
b. When the first wish made the poor man rich, he wished to be on a tropical island. He found himself on a deserted island with nowhere to spend his money. So he had to waste his last wish coming home. *Deduction AF3*
c. The reference to leprechauns burying a jar of coins 'at the foot of a rainbow' and to them granting wishes shows that they are fictional creatures. *Inference AF3*
d. *Personal opinion AF7*

BEYOND THE RECORD

Research another creature from folklore. Write a character sketch for this creature.

Background research, reading and discussion to help the children to prepare

- Ask the children to name other creatures from folklore that they already know. Write a list on the board.
- Revise the structure of a character sketch, using the reading comprehension text as an exemplar.
- Guide children to books or websites to carry out more detailed research of their chosen creature, e.g. http://en.wikipedia.org/wiki/List_of_legendary_creatures_by_type.

Recording their ideas

- Will the children make notes as they read text, or create a Mind Map™ with a branch for each sub-heading to be included in their character sketch?
- Will the children illustrate their character sketch? Will they create a drawing of their mythical creature or find an image from the internet and credit the source?

Feedback: Encourage children to swap their character sketches and provide constructive feedback about what has been done well and what could be improved.

LANGUAGE ACTIVITY WORKSHEET

- Ask the children what they understand by the term *mischievous*.
- Provide them with copies of the worksheet and ask them to write synonyms for *mischievous* on the spidergram. Provide the children with a dictionary and thesaurus to help them find the words and definitions.

Possible answers: naughty, playful, impish, roguish, bad, ill-behaved.

NAME:　　　　　　　　　　　　　　　　　　　　　　　　DATE:

MISCHIEF-MAKERS

Words that have the same or similar meanings are called synonyms.
For example, *mischievous* and *troublesome* are synonyms.

How many other synonyms can you find for *mischievous*?

Add the words to the spidergram. Include a short definition for each word. You can use a dictionary or thesaurus to help you.

mischievous
Definition: causing trouble in a playful way.

Definition:

Definition:

Definition:

Definition:

Definition:

Definition:

© Rising Stars UK Ltd. 2013　　　Comprehension/Year 5/Largest gathering of people dressed as leprechauns

GUINNESS WORLD RECORDS

RECORD-BREAKING COMPREHENSION – YEAR 5

MOST DECKS OF PLAYING CARDS MEMORISED – SINGLE SIGHTING

This web page provides tips and strategies for improving memory. The text features information about the Guinness World Record for the most decks of playing cards memorised on a single sighting.

Text type:	instructions
AFs covered:	AF2, AF3, AF4, AF5
Specialist vocabulary:	technique, visualise, acrostic, memorable, sequence

ON YOUR MARKS

a. Dave Farrow comes from Canada. *Literal AF2*
b. A ridiculous image is more likely to stick in your mind and will help you remember what you associated it with. *Inference AF3*
c. To remember the order of a group of things, you might 'acrostic it'. *Deduction AF3*
d. The phrase means that the more ridiculous the image, the more likely you are to remember it. *Deduction AF3*

GET SET

a. To help you remember a long number, you could 'chunk it'. *Literal AF2*
b. The web page advises you to practise using the memory techniques. *Deduction AF3*
c. Words and phrases that tell you this is a set of instructions include the command words 'visualise', 'picture', 'chain', 'chunk', 'group', 'create' and the phrase 'If you practise these techniques'. *Inference AF4, AF5*
d. *Personal opinion AF3*

GO FOR GOLD!

a. An acrostic sentence is made up of words that begin with the initial letters of what you want to remember. *Literal AF2, AF3*
b. The drawback is that you might forget the acrostic sentence, or you might remember it in the wrong order. *Inference AF3*
c. In the acrostic sentence in the web page, Mercury and Mars begin with the same letter so you could put them in the wrong order. *Deduction AF3*
d. The web page tells you that having a good memory can be a benefit because you will find it easier to remember people's names, lists of numbers, and other facts. *Personal opinion/inference AF3*

BEYOND THE RECORD

Use the information in the web page to create a three-minute presentation entitled 'Brain training tips'. What key information will you include?

Background research, reading and discussion to help the children to prepare

- Talk about the audience for the presentation. Will it be for other children in the class, younger children in the school, or perhaps parents or governors? What difference will the audience make to the language used in the presentation? What information will keep the audience interested?
- Talk about the time available for the presentation and the effect this will have on the amount of information that can be presented. Discuss the importance of talking slowly and clearly.

Recording their ideas

- How will the children select the key information from the reading comprehension text? Will they highlight the important information or make notes in the margin?
- How will the children structure their presentation? Will they write a script by hand or on the computer and hold up visual aids for the audience, or create a PowerPoint® presentation that can be projected onto a whiteboard?

LANGUAGE ACTIVITY WORKSHEET

- Explain that an acrostic can be useful as a mnemonic for remembering spellings.
- Write some acrostics on the whiteboard as examples, e.g. PUPIL – pick up pencils in lines; RHYTHM – rhythm helps your two hips move.
- Provide the children with the worksheet and read the words together.
- Ask the children to invent acrostic sentences to help them remember how to spell each word. Share their acrostics with the class.

NAME: DATE:

ACROSTIC SPELLINGS

Acrostics can help us to remember sentences, phrases and spellings.
Big Elephants Can Always Understand Small Elephants is an acrostic for the word *because*.

GUINNESS WORLD RECORDS — OFFICIALLY AMAZING

Work out your own acrostics to help you remember how to spell these words.

1. blemish _____

2. coward _____

3. equip _____

4. length _____

5. nation _____

6. wrench _____

Now create three more acrostics for words that you find difficult to spell.

1. _____

2. _____

3. _____

© Rising Stars UK Ltd. 2013   Record-Breaking Comprehension/Year 5/Most decks of playing cards memorised – single sighting

GUINNESS WORLD RECORDS

RECORD-BREAKING COMPREHENSION – YEAR 5

LARGEST TORCHLIT PARADE

This page from a travel magazine explores torchlit parades from around the world, including the Annual Freedom Celebration in Indonesia, which holds the Guinness World Record for the largest torchlit parade.

Text type:	explanation
AFs covered:	AF2, AF3, AF5
Specialist vocabulary:	celebration, procession, hessian, occasion, elaborate, flambeaux

ON YOUR MARKS

a. Torchlit parades are usually held at night. *Literal AF2*
b. The Olympic Torch parade is held once every four years because the Olympic Games are held every four years. *Deduction AF3*
c. People mark the opening or closing of events with torchlit parades to help make them memorable. *Inference, personal opinion AF3*
d. If a lighted torch had no protection, the hot wax might drip onto your hand and burn you. *Inference AF3*

GET SET

a. The torches are made with wax or from hessian cloth rolled into a tube and soaked in wax. *Literal AF2*
b. The word 'aloft' means high up, in this case above people's heads. *Deduction AF5*
c. When torches are thrown into a wooden Viking boat, the boat is set on fire. *Inference AF3*
d. The Olympic Torch parade is the most famous because most countries of the world take part in the Olympic Games. *Inference AF3*

GO FOR GOLD!

a. 'Flambeaux' means lighted torch in French. *Literal AF2*
b. The author describes the Up Helly Aa parade as spectacular because of the parade of men and boys dressed up as Vikings and carrying flaming torches, and the torches being thrown into a Viking boat, which must be exciting to see. *Deduction AF5*
c. A relay of runners is used to carry the Olympic flame because it travels all the way from Greece and is too far for one person to carry. *Inference AF3*
d. *Personal opinion*

BEYOND THE RECORD

Imagine you want to be an Olympic torchbearer in the next Olympic Games. Write a persuasive letter to apply to take part in the Torch relay.

Background research, reading and discussion to help the children to prepare

- If possible, watch some video clips of the torch relay from the 2012 London Olympics.
- With the children, discuss why people want to take part in the Olympic Torch relay and write ideas on the whiteboard.
- Talk about what the decision-maker might be looking for in a torch bearer, for example achievements and charity work.

Checklist for persuasive letter writing:

- Layout.
- Formal language.
- Explain the reasons why they are the best choice.
- Use catchy phrases to grab attention.

LANGUAGE ACTIVITY WORKSHEET

- Use this worksheet to look at how hyphens can be used to avoid ambiguity. Point to the definition and example at the top of the worksheet. Discuss how the use of a hyphen changes the meaning of the phrase.
- Explain that the activity on the worksheet gives the children six phrases that they need to re-write as hyphenated adjectival phrases.
- Once the children have completed the worksheet, encourage them to research more examples of hyphenated phrases.

Answers: male-only, world-famous, first-time, easy-to-hold, fair-haired, wax-soaked.

NAME: DATE:

FLAMING HYPHENS

Sometimes two words next to each other can have two different meanings and confuse the reader when put in a sentence.
We can use hyphens (-) to make the meaning clear.
The boys were ten years old
The ten-year-old boys

Change these phrases using a hyphen to link the adjectives for clarity.
An example is given below.

1. A parade of only men. A _____-_____ parade.

2. Mardi Gras is famous throughout the world. Mardi Gras is _____-_____ .

3. Visitors for the first time. _____-_____ visitors.

4. The torches are easy to hold. The _____-_____-_____ torches.

5. Vikings had fair hair. The _____-_____ Vikings.

6. The hessian was soaked in wax. The _____-_____ hessian.

Now write three hyphenated phrases of your own.

1. _____

_____

2. _____

_____

3. _____

_____

© Rising Stars UK Ltd. 2013   Record-Breaking Comprehension/Year 5/Largest torchlit parade

GUINNESS WORLD RECORDS

RECORD-BREAKING COMPREHENSION – YEAR 5

LONGEST FINGERNAILS (FEMALE) – EVER

This text, based on the Guinness World Record for the longest fingernails (female) – ever, is in the form of an email from one girl to another before they meet up to get their nails painted.

Text type:	biography
AFs covered:	AF2, AF3, AF5
Specialist vocabulary:	incredible, appreciate, feature, officially, injuries, interview

ANSWERS

ON YOUR MARKS

a. Lee Redmond started growing her nails in 1979. *Literal AF2*
b. Putting on a heavy coat with such long nails would be difficult because it would be hard to get the nails through the sleeves without breaking them. The long nails could also tear or damage the coat. *Deduction AF3*
c. Examples of informal language are 'loads of media attention', 'Check out the photo I've pasted below', 'Can you believe it?' (any of these answers is acceptable). *Deduction AF5*
d. *Personal opinion AF3*

GET SET

a. Lee Redmond's nails were measured on an Italian TV show called *Lo Show dei Record* on 23 February 2008. *Literal AF2*
b. 'Media attention' means being interviewed and photographed by newspapers, magazines, radio and TV. *Deduction AF5*
c. She still holds the Guinness World Record because no one else has yet grown longer nails. *Inference AF3*
d. *Personal opinion AF3*

GO FOR GOLD!

a. Lee Redmond comes from Salt Lake City, USA. *Literal AF2*
b. Lee Redmond meant that her hands felt lighter and moved much more quickly. *Deduction AF5*
c. Sonya might 'appreciate' this Guinness World Record because she is planning on getting her nails painted and so she probably likes to take care of her nails. *Deduction AF3*
d. Bella calls Lee 'an incredible lady' because she still managed to carry on with day-to-day activities and care for her ill husband when she had very long nails. *Inference AF3, AF5*

BEYOND THE RECORD

What would your day be like with very long fingernails? Write a list of your everyday activities, such as cleaning your teeth and getting dressed. Create a scale and grade each activity on your list from easy to impossible.

Background research, reading and discussion to help the children to prepare

- Working in small groups, ask children to discuss and write down activities that they do every day, such as cleaning their teeth, combing their hair, eating meals, etc.
- Bring the class back together and look at the picture of Lee Redmond in the reading comprehension text. Ask the children to imagine they have very long fingernails like Lee Redmond and are trying to undertake each of the tasks on their list.

Recording their ideas

- What kind of scale will the children use to grade each activity? Will they use a numbered scale, words or colours?
- Encourage each group to compare their ideas and discuss any differences.

LANGUAGE ACTIVITY WORKSHEET

- Remind the children how compound words are formed.
- Ask them to scan the reading comprehension text to find any compound words (examples are *fingernails*, *newspaper* and *grandchildren*).
- Provide the children with the worksheet and ask them to use the words in the boxes to form compound words.
- Fast finishers can move on to use some of the compound words in a paragraph about Lee Redmond.

Possible answers: fingernail, fingerprint, fingertip; newspaper, newsprint, newsreader; website, webpage.

NAME: DATE:

COMPOUND WORDS
Compound words are made by combining two smaller words to make one new word.

How many compound words can you make by joining one word from each box?

| finger |
| news |
| web |

| paper | nail | site |
| print | reader | page | tip |

Write the compound words below.

_____

_____

_____

Now use three of the compound words to write a paragraph about Lee Redmond.

© Rising Stars UK Ltd. 2013   Record-Breaking Comprehension/Year 5/Longest fingernails (female) – ever

GUINNESS WORLD RECORDS

RECORD-BREAKING COMPREHENSION – YEAR 5

SHORTEST LIVING WOMAN

This text, in the form of a magazine article, focuses on Jyoti Amge, who holds the Guinness World Record for the shortest living woman. The text explores her ambitions and aspirations.

Text type:	biography
AFs covered:	AF2, AF3, AF5, AF6
Specialist vocabulary:	muscular, aspiring, dwarfism, presence, recognised, announcement, ambition

ON YOUR MARKS

a. The shortest woman in the world is Jyoti Amge. *Literal AF2*
b. 'Aspiring to look the same as someone else' means wishing you looked like another person. *Deduction AF5*
c. Jyoti was crying because she felt emotional/happy to receive the Guinness World Record. *Inference AF3*
d. *Personal opinion AF3*

GET SET

a. Jyoti wants to be an actress in Bollywood. *Literal AF2*
b. The author is trying to make it clear that regardless of your size, it is possible to achieve your goals and to live a happy and fulfilling life. *Inference AF6*
c. 'Press presence' means lots of news reporters and photographers. *Deduction AF5*
d. The author wants you to admire Jyoti and does this by using positive phrases about her. Examples include: 'The shortest woman in the world … shows that regardless of our size or shape, everyone can achieve their goals and live happy and fulfilling lives' and 'Jyoti is certainly a shining example of how being different should not affect what we can achieve in life'. *Inference AF6*

GO FOR GOLD!

a. 'But' is the connective word used in the fourth paragraph. *Literal AF2*
b. The name for this type of recount is a biography. *Deduction AF3*
c. The author used the word 'shining' to show that Jyoti lives up to the meaning of her name. *Inference AF5*
d. Jyoti was not treated differently because of her size when she was at school, but she was treated differently on her 18th birthday because there were lots of newspaper reporters asking her questions and photographers taking her picture. *Personal opinion, Inference AF3*

BEYOND THE RECORD

Use three internet sources to find out more about Jyoti Amge. Imagine Jyoti is travelling from India to visit your school. What three questions would you ask her that you cannot answer from your internet research?

Background research, reading and discussion to help the children to prepare

- Ask the children to re-read the reading comprehension text. What information would they like to know about Jyoti that they cannot find in the text?
- Guide the children to sources such as http://en.wikipedia.org/wiki/Jyoti_Amge. If possible, watch a video clip of Jyoti. Be aware of inappropriate advertising and comments on websites such as YouTube; try to select a video clip in advance.

Recording their ideas

- How will the children record their ideas for questions?
- Encourage them to write up to 10 questions and then select the best three. How will they select the best questions?
- Can they team up with another pair or group to role-play the interview?

Ideas for questions may include: How do you feel about being famous? How did you feel when you broke the Guinness World Record? Who do you admire the most?

LANGUAGE ACTIVITY WORKSHEET

- Ask the children to scan the text to find what Jyoti said to the reporters at the Guinness World Records ceremony. Explain that this is an indirect quotation.
- Discuss the difference between direct and indirect quotations with the children.
- Ask the children to rewrite the indirect quotations as direct quotations. Remind them to use speech punctuation and to check the verb tenses.

Answers: 'I wasn't treated differently,' said Jyoti; I want to be a Bollywood actress,' Jyoti told us; 'I am pursuing a career in politics,' said Jyoti; 'I am pleased and proud to hold the Guinness World Record,' Jyoti told the press.

NAME: DATE:

DIRECT QUOTATIONS

A direct quotation tells us exactly what a person has said. An indirect quote paraphrases what someone said.

'This is an extra birthday present,' said Jyoti tearfully. (direct quotation)

Jyoti tearfully told reporters that this was an 'extra birthday present'. (indirect quotation)

The magazine article uses indirect quotations about Jyoti. Rewrite these as direct quotations using the correct tense and punctuation.

Jyoti said that she wasn't treated differently.

_____

_____

Jyoti told us that she wants to be a Bollywood actress.

_____

_____

Jyoti said that she is pursuing a career in politics.

_____

_____

Jyoti told the press that she is pleased and proud to hold the Guinness World Record.

_____

_____

Now imagine you are a newspaper reporter. Use one of the direct quotations to write a short news summary of what happened on Jyoti's 18th birthday.

_____

_____

_____

_____

_____

© Rising Stars UK Ltd. 2013   Record-Breaking Comprehension/Year 5/Shortest living woman

GUINNESS WORLD RECORDS

RECORD-BREAKING COMPREHENSION – YEAR 5

LARGEST DRUMMING LESSON

This text, in the style of a newsletter for teachers, is based on the Guinness World Record for the largest drumming lesson. It describes how to create simple rhythms and recounts the largest drumming lesson.

Text type:	recount
AFs covered:	AF2, AF3, AF5, AF6
Specialist vocabulary:	professional, rhythm, surface, session, celebrate diversity, participant, technique, principle, sequence, atmosphere, unique, experience

ON YOUR MARKS

a. The largest drumming lesson took place at Chessington World of Adventures in Surrey. *Literal AF2*
b. You don't need to be a professional drummer because all you need is a surface to beat. *Deduction AF2*
c. Having a good teacher would make 'all the difference' because he or she would be able to pass on his/her expertise and enthusiasm to help you to improve your skills. *Inference AF3*
d. This particular event was organised to mark Africa Day because the children used traditional African drums to break a Guinness World Record. *Inference, personal opinion AF3*

GET SET

a. The largest drumming lesson lasted 30 minutes. *Literal AF2*
b. The author wants to encourage events like this because he/she writes enthusiastically about the event using exclamation marks and language such as 'celebrates', 'success' and 'unique experience'. *Inference AF6*
c. 'Drumming techniques' means different ways to make sounds on a drum. *Inference AF3, AF5*
d. *Personal opinion AF3*

GO FOR GOLD!

a. The word in the text that means 'variety' is 'diversity'. *Deduction AF2*
b. The children and teachers played traditional African drums because they are simple to learn and the event was to mark Africa Day. *Deduction AF3*
c. It was very important for everyone to drum the same rhythm during the performance so that the rhythm was clear and sounded impressive. *Inference AF3*
d. *Personal opinion AF3*

BEYOND THE RECORD

Use three different sources to find out more about different kinds of traditional drums from around the world, including where they are from and how they are played. Create an information sheet for three of these drums.

Background research, reading and discussion to help the children to prepare

- With the class, look at websites such as www.worldmusicalinstruments.com/c-9-world-drums.aspx and http://en.wikipedia.org/wiki/Drum to highlight the variety of drums from around the world. With the children, draw up a list of up to 10 types of drum on the board.
- Encourage the children to use a safe internet search to find out more information about their favourite three drums.

Recording their ideas

- How will the children present their information? As an alphabetical guide, encyclopedia of drums, paragraphs with sub-headings?
- Will the children use photos or illustrations? (Ensure they acknowledge the source of any online images.)

Feedback: Encourage the children to share their work with others. Is the information accessible and interesting? Would they do anything differently next time?

LANGUAGE ACTIVITY WORKSHEET

- This worksheet investigates the effect of a passive voice in a text. Point out the example at the top of the page. If necessary, give some more examples.
- Discuss the different emphasis when the statements have a passive voice compared to an active voice.
- Point out the use of a passive voice in other texts, e.g. formal language texts.

Answers: African diversity and success was celebrated on Africa Day, Drums were played by 242 children, They were taught how to warm up by a teacher, The same rhythm was drummed by 260 people, The experience was enjoyed by children and staff alike.

NAME: DATE:

ACTIVE TO PASSIVE

We can change the effect and emphasis of a sentence by using a passive voice instead of an active voice.

Active voice: The participants used African drums.
Passive voice: African drums were used by the participants.

Change these sentences from the active voice to the passive voice.

Active	Passive
The participants used African drums.	*African drums were used by the participants.*
Africa Day celebrated African diversity and success.	
242 children played the drums.	
A teacher taught them how to warm up.	
260 people drummed the same rhythm.	
Children and staff alike enjoyed the experience.	

© Rising Stars UK Ltd. 2013   Record-Breaking Comprehension/Year 5/Largest drumming lesson

GUINNESS WORLD RECORDS

RECORD-BREAKING COMPREHENSION – YEAR 5

DEEPEST SCUBA DIVE IN SEA WATER

This magazine recount is about Nuno Gomes who, on 10 June 2005, broke the Guinness World Record for the deepest scuba dive in sea water.

Text type:	recount
AFs covered:	AF2, AF3, AF7
Specialist vocabulary:	scuba, oxygen, buoy, decompression, pressure, diver

ON YOUR MARKS

a. Nuno dived to a depth of 318.25 m. *Literal AF2*
b. At the end of his dive, Nuno would have felt very tired, but happy that he had broken the Guinness World Record. *Deduction AF3*
c. Nuno needed a team to help keep him safe. *Inference AF3*
d. People who go diving or are interested in diving would read this article because it is in a diving magazine. *Inference AF3*

GET SET

a. Nuno set his world record in the Red Sea off Dahab, Egypt. *Literal AF2*
b. The *NABQ Explorer* is the boat that Nuno and his team used for the dive. *Deduction AF3*
c. The message label 'OK' meant that Nuno was still feeling OK at that stage of the dive. *Deduction AF3*
d. *Personal opinion AF3*

GO FOR GOLD!

a. Nuno had to bring back special labels as proof that he had broken the record. *Literal AF2*
b. The long weighted line guided Nuno safely to the seabed to prevent him getting lost. *Inference AF3*
c. The main danger was rising to the surface too quickly after diving so far down. A quick change in air pressure is called 'decompression' or 'the bends' and can be fatal. *Inference AF3*
d. *Personal opinion AF7*

BEYOND THE RECORD

Write five questions you would like to ask Nuno. In pairs, take it in turns to be Nuno and the person asking him questions. When you are playing the role of interviewer, make a note of the answers that 'Nuno' gives.

Background research, reading and discussion to help the children to prepare

- Search online for information about deep-sea scuba diving and its risks, e.g. www.allthesea.com/Deep-Sea-Diving.html.
- Provide websites about Nuno, e.g. www.nunogomes.co.za/
- Discuss how to scan sources and texts for ideas.

Recording their ideas

- Encourage the children to decide how to record their ideas for questions: a simple list, sticky notes, a Mind Map™?
- How will they sequence their questions? Chronologically, in no obvious sequence?
- How will they record the answers? By recording the interview and writing down the answers afterwards; writing down answers during the interview; by the 'interviewee' writing them down?

Ideas for questions may include: decompression risks and methods to overcome them, the attractions of deep-sea diving, equipment, his thoughts and feelings as he dives, future projects.

LANGUAGE ACTIVITY WORKSHEET

- The worksheet allows the children to work on words with endings sounding like *zhuh* (*-sure*) and *chuh* (*-ture*). Point out that words ending *(t)ch* with *-er*, e.g. *teacher* or *catcher*, do not end with *-ture*.
- Ask the children to add the correct ending to the labels going down the two diver lines. They should then complete one more *-sure* word and *-ture* word and write them in the correct boxes. Make sure the children have access to dictionaries – paper or online.
- Once they have completed the worksheet, discuss with the children how knowing the sounds and patterns for these words can help with their spelling and reading.

Answers: treasure, picture, creature, measure, capture, pressure, nature, pleasure. Possible answers for words ending in *sure* and *ture* are leisure and rapture.

NAME: DATE:

DEEP-SEA SPELLING

Words with endings that sound like *zhuh* are spelled *-sure*.   enclosure
Words with endings that sound like *chuh* are spelled *-ture*.   departure

Add in the correct *-sure* or *-ture* endings to the word labels on the diver lines.

Add your own two words in the bottom boxes.

trea_____

pic_____

crea_____

cap_____

mea_____

pres_____

_____ sure

na_____

plea_____

_____ ture

Now use four of these words to write a paragraph about diving in the sea.

_____
_____
_____
_____
_____

© Rising Stars UK Ltd. 2013   Record-Breaking Comprehension/Year 5/Deepest scuba dive in sea water

GUINNESS WORLD RECORDS

RECORD-BREAKING COMPREHENSION – YEAR 5

STRANGEST DIET

This text describes the extraordinary talent of Michel Lotito, who was famous for consuming metal. He holds the Guinness World Record for the strangest diet.

Text type:	biography
AFs covered:	AF2, AF3, AF5, AF6
Specialist vocabulary:	entertainer, Monsieur Mangetout, average, Grenoble, bizarre, amusement, consumed, chandeliers, Eiffel

ON YOUR MARKS

a. Michel Lotito was born in Grenoble. *Literal AF2*
b. 'Natural causes' means that Michel Lotito did not die because of long-term illness or injury (for example, from eating metal). *Deduction AF5*
c. His skill is described as 'rare' because so few people eat metal *Deduction AF3, AF5*
d. Personal opinion *AF3*

GET SET

a. On average, Michel Lotito ate 900 g of metal a day. *Literal AF2*
b. The oil and water helped him by making his throat slippery to help him swallow. *Inference AF3*
c. Eating metal could be harmful because the sharp edges might puncture your insides or cause a blockage in your digestive system. *Personal opinion, deduction AF3*
d. 'Food' and 'meal' are in quotation marks as the metal he ate is not a recognised food or meal. *Inference AF5*

GO FOR GOLD!

a. He ate 15 shopping trolleys. *Literal AF2*
b. It took two years to eat the Cessna because it was an aeroplane so there was a lot of metal to consume. *Deduction AF3*
c. The author wants the reader to find the sub-heading amusing – it is ironic. *Inference AF5, AF6*
d. The author included the 'coffin inside a man' comment because this is a reversal of what normally happens and so very interesting information and is entertaining to the reader. *Personal opinion, inference AF6*

BEYOND THE RECORD

Write 100 words summarising the life achievements of someone from history.

Background research, reading and discussion to help the children to prepare

- As a class, brainstorm some interesting people throughout history. Write a list on the board for children to refer back to. Ask the children to choose someone from history that interests them and research key facts about his or her life using the internet or books.
- Briefly go through the features of a biography. Discus the length of the biography that the children need to write and how they need to record important facts and events concisely.

Recording their ideas

- How will the children choose the most important information? Through discussion, elimination of less important information, rewriting sentences to be more precise?
- Will the biographies be presented as a short fact file with sub-headings as short paragraphs, as a timeline with captions?

Feedback: Encourage the children to share their biographies. Are they easy to read; do they contain biographical features? What could be improved?

LANGUAGE ACTIVITY WORKSHEET

- Use this worksheet to help reinforce learning the spellings and difference in meaning of homophones. Remind the children what a homophone is and give a few examples.
- Ask the children to insert the correct homophones into the headlines.
- Encourage the children to write two more headlines using the two pairs of remaining homophones.

Answers: Rare herd of cattle heard to have escaped; Pudding from the Gobi desert deemed a delicious dessert; Woolly jumper! Ewe found in yew tree; Master baker creates exquisite dough in the shape of a doe; Stationery supplies low as freezing roads keep lorries stationary; Rain downpour won't stop queen's reign.

NAME: **DATE:**

MIXING UP HOMOPHONES

Homophones are words that sound the same but have different meanings.
piece: a part that has been taken from something whole
peace: freedom from conflict

Write the correct homophones in the headlines using the words in the box.

Rare _____ of cattle _____ to have escaped

Pudding from the Gobi _____ deemed a delicious _____

Woolly jumper! _____ found in _____ tree

Master baker creates exquisite _____ in the shape of a _____

_____ supplies low as freezing roads keep lorries _____

_____ downpour won't stop queen's _____

| dessert | stationery | practice | doe | rain | reign | heard | place |
| desert | ewe | stationary | plaice | dough | herd | yew | practise |

Write two of your own headlines using the four remaining homophones.

_____

_____

© Rising Stars UK Ltd. 2013   Record-Breaking Comprehension/Year 5/Strangest diet

GUINNESS WORLD RECORDS

RECORD-BREAKING COMPREHENSION – YEAR 5

LARGEST GYMNASTIC DISPLAY (FEMALE)

This page from an in-flight magazine explores the attractions and practicalities of Pyongyang, the capital of North Korea (the Democratic People's Republic of Korea). It is based on the Guinness World Record for the largest gymnastic display set in August 2007.

Text type:	non-chronological report
AFs covered:	AF2, AF3, AF5, AF6
Specialist vocabulary:	mysterious, Communist, destination, tourists, commemorate, resistance, liberation, Arc de Triomphe, monument, gigantic, process, authorities

ON YOUR MARKS

a. Pyongyang is the capital city of the DPRK. *Literal AF2*
b. If you apply for a visa well in advance, you are more likely to receive it in time for your trip. *Deduction AF3*
c. Most visiting tourists come from China because it is close to the DPRK and is another Communist country. *Deduction AF3*
d. 'Must-see event' means an event that is so good you cannot afford to miss it. *Inference AF5*

GET SET

a. The Arirang Mass Games is held in the May Day Stadium, Pyongyang. *Literal AF2*
b. The verb 'commemorate' means to mark an occasion or remember an event, people or a person. *Deduction AF5*
c. The DPRK is a holiday destination 'like no other' because it is one of the last remaining Communist countries in the world and, unlike other holiday destinations, local guides will accompany you when you visit any of the tourist sites. *Inference AF3*
d. Personal opinion *AF6*

GO FOR GOLD!

a. The May Day Stadium holds 150,000 spectators. *Literal AF2*
b. The country names are abbreviated because they are long and take up space. The text is also easier to read when the names are abbreviated. *Deduction AF3*
c. The author could have abbreviated the name of the committee that organised the record attempt. *Deduction AF3*
d. Personal opinion *AF3*

BEYOND THE RECORD

Use the internet to research unusual holiday destinations. What destination would you most like to visit? Describe the destination, say why it is unusual and why you would like to visit.

Background research, reading and discussion to help the children to prepare

- As a class, discuss unusual holiday destinations. Has anyone in the class been somewhere unusual on their holidays? If possible, project a map of the world on the board, or provide children with atlases for reference.
- Guide children to websites such as www.101holidays.co.uk/unusual-holidays/ and www.responsibletravel.com/holidays/unusual to research a range of unusual destinations. You may want to suggest that children focus on destinations in one continent.

Recording their ideas

- How will the children structure their information? With a framework of sub-headings, or one major heading with content split into paragraphs?
- Will children include images or maps of their destination?

Feedback: Ask the children to share their destinations with each other and discuss their choices and the reasons for them.

LANGUAGE ACTIVITY WORKSHEET

- Ask the children to find the word *gigantic* in the text and say what it means.
- Remind children of the definition of a synonym. Ask them to think of as many synonyms for *gigantic* as they can, and to write a sentence using each one. Fast finishers can use a thesaurus to list even more synonyms.
- Ask the children to share their synonyms and sentences with each other.

Possible answers: enormous, colossal, huge, massive, big, vast, large, gargantuan.

NAME: DATE:

GIGANTIC DISPLAY

Words that have the same or similar meanings are called synonyms.

OFFICIALLY AMAZING

In the text, the May Day Stadium is described as *gigantic*.

How many synonyms can you think of for *gigantic*? Write them in the spaces below.

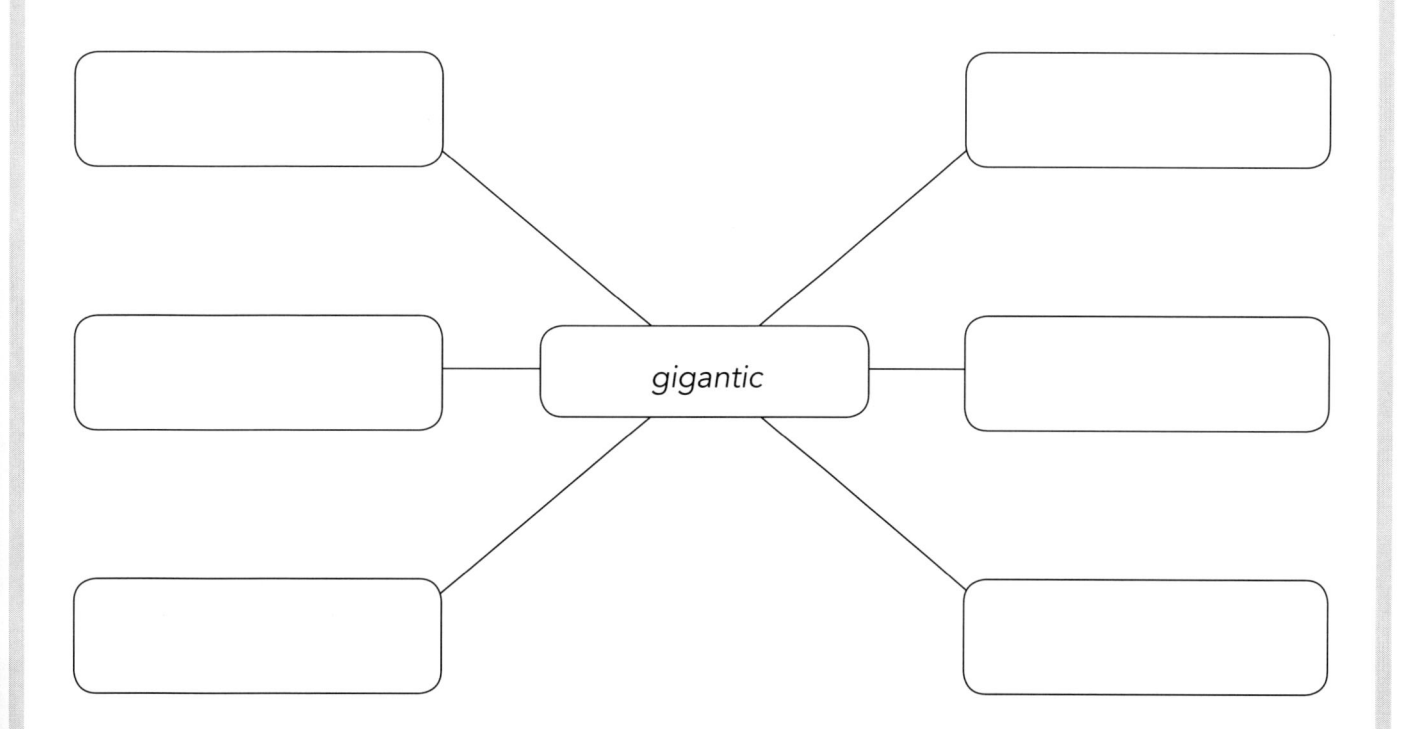

gigantic

Now write a sentence using each synonym.

1. _____
2. _____
3. _____
4. _____
5. _____
6. _____

© Rising Stars UK Ltd. 2013   Record-Breaking Comprehension/Year 5/Largest gymnastic display (female)

GUINNESS WORLD RECORDS

RECORD-BREAKING COMPREHENSION – YEAR 5

LARGEST ATLAS

This text, in the form of a web page, explores the history of map-making. The text includes information about the Guinness World Record for the largest atlas.

Text type:	non-chronological report
AFs covered:	AF2, AF3, AF5
Specialist vocabulary:	cartographer, navigator, dimensional, Millennium, measure, library, estimated, professional, photographer

ON YOUR MARKS

a. An atlas is a collection of maps in the form of a book. *Literal AF2*
b. 'Two-dimensional' is the hyphenated term used in the text to mean 'flat'. *Deduction AF3, AF5*
c. An atlas is a collection of maps in a two-dimensional form. A globe is spherical and shows the world in a three-dimensional form. *Deduction AF3*
d. Only 31 copies of Earth Platinum were printed because not many people would need such a large atlas, or would be able to afford it. *Inference AF3*

GET SET

a. A cartographer creates maps. *Literal AF2*
b. Earth Platinum is so expensive because it would cost a lot to print such a big book; over 100 professionals worked on it and had to be paid. *Inference AF3*
c. Modern cartographers have aerial photography, satellites and computers to help them create maps. *Deduction AF3*
d. People wanted to 'find their way around the Earth' in the 1500s to explore new places and to trade goods with other countries. *Inference AF3*

GO FOR GOLD!

a. People started to create maps in the Iron Age. *Literal AF2*
b. The word 'seamless' literally means 'without a seam'. In the text it means unbroken and continuous. *Deduction AF3, AF5*
c. Satellite images are used because they are photographs taken of the Earth from space and so are completely accurate. *Inference AF3*
d. Personal opinion *AF3*

BEYOND THE RECORD

Create a map to help visitors find their way around your school. Use a key to explain the different features of your map.

Background research, reading and discussion to help the children to prepare

- Suggest that a map of the school would be useful to give to visitors when they are trying to find their way around.
- If possible, show some examples of maps from tourist attractions, either on a printed leaflet or online. What features do these maps have in common?
- Will the children create a map of the school buildings only, or include the rest of the school grounds? If time is limited, the children could create a more detailed map of their classroom.

Recording their ideas

- Will the children use a key with symbols, or colours, to highlight specific features such as toilets or classrooms?
- Will the children create their map on paper, or use a design tool on the computer?

Feedback: Encourage children to share their maps and use any feedback to improve them.

LANGUAGE ACTIVITY WORKSHEET

- This worksheet can be used to revise the effect of passive voice in a text. Point out the example at the top of the page. If necessary, give more examples until the children are confident about the idea of passive and active voice.
- Ask them to look through the text and find examples of active sentences.
- Provide children with the worksheet and ask them to change the active sentences to passive sentences. Fast finishers can create their own active and passive sentence about map-making.

Answers: Maps are created by a cartographer, The term 'atlas' was first used by Mercator, The largest atlas was published by Millennium House, The atlas was created by 100 professionals, A single, seamless, image was created by special photographic techniques.

NAME: _____ DATE: _____

PASSIVE VERBS

Changing a sentence from active to passive changes the emphasis from the subject to the object of the sentence.

Active voice: The man (subject) opened the atlas (object).
Passive voice: The atlas (object) was opened by the man (subject).

Change these active sentences into passive sentences.

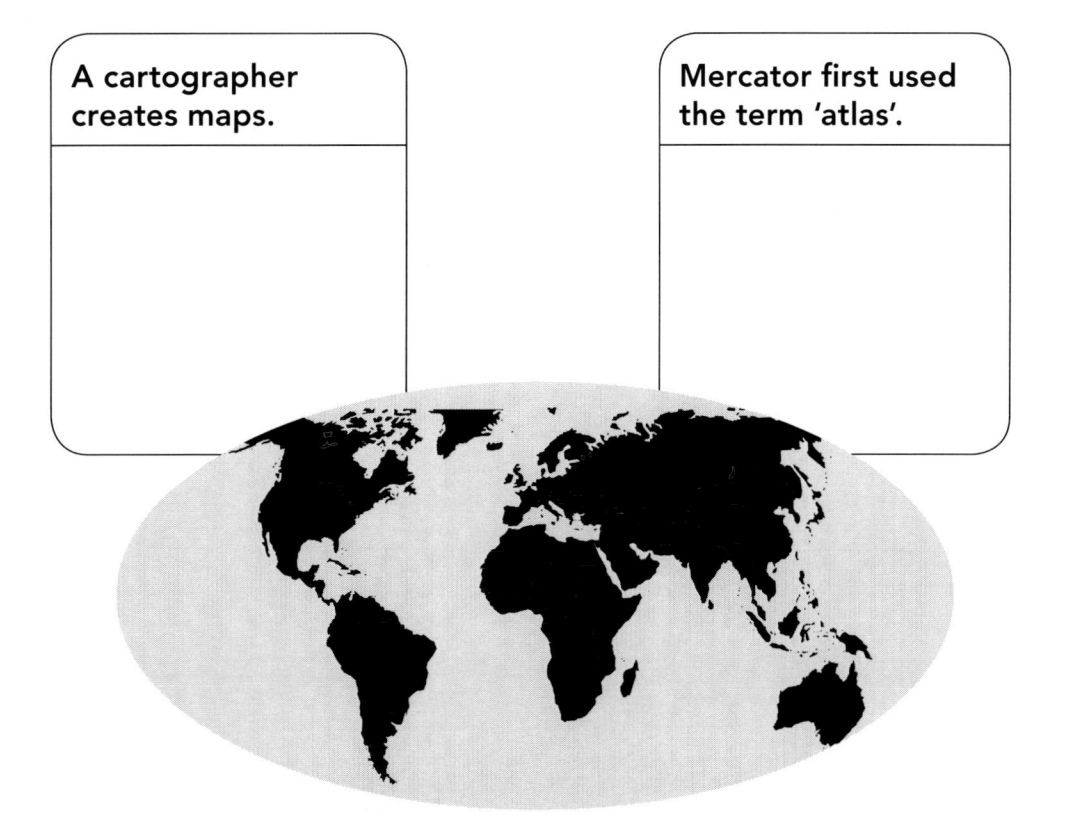

- A cartographer creates maps.
- Mercator first used the term 'atlas'.
- Millennium House published the largest atlas.
- 100 professionals created the atlas.
- Special photographic techniques created a single, seamless image.

Now create your own active and passive sentence about map-making.

Active: _____

Passive: _____

© Rising Stars UK Ltd. 2013   Record-Breaking Comprehension/Year 5/Largest atlas

GUINNESS WORLD RECORDS

RECORD-BREAKING COMPREHENSION – YEAR 5

NOTES

Use this page to make notes about the reading comprehension texts and activities or any topic/subject links with your curriculum to share with other class teachers.